JESUS' PROCLAMATION
OF
THE KINGDOM OF GOD

Lives of Jesus Series

LEANDER E. KECK, General Editor

JESUS' PROCLAMATION
OF
THE KINGDOM OF GOD

by

JOHANNES WEISS

*Translated, edited
and with an
Introduction by*

RICHARD HYDE HIERS
and
DAVID LARRIMORE HOLLAND

BT
94
W3813

FORTRESS PRESS

Philadelphia

This book is a translation of *Die Predigt Jesu vom Reiche Gottes* (First edition; Göttingen: Vandenhoeck & Ruprecht, 1892).

Library of Congress Catalog Card Number 79-135267

ISBN 0-8006-0153-X

1405G70   Printed in U.S.A.   1-153

CONTENTS

ABBREVIATIONS

HTR: Harvard Theological Review

JAAR: Journal of the American Academy of Religion

JBL: Journal of Biblical Literature

JBR: Journal of Bible and Religion

JR: Journal of Religion

JTS: Journal of Theological Studies

NT: Novum Testamentum

NTS: New Testament Studies

RGG: Die Religion in Geschichte und Gegenwart

SBT: Studies in Biblical Theology

SJT: Scottish Journal of Theology

Strack-Billerbeck: H. L. Strack and P. Billerbeck, Kommentar zum N.T. aus Talmud und Midrasch (1-4, 1922-28)

TSK: Theologische Studien und Kritiken

ZNW: Zeitschrift für die neutestamentliche Wissenschaft

ZThK: Zeitschrift für Theologie und Kirche

FOREWORD
TO THE SERIES

In a time when a premium is placed on experimentation for the future and when theological work itself values "new theology," the reasons for reissuing theological works from the past are not self-evident. Above all, there is broad consensus that the "Lives of Jesus" produced by our forebears failed both as sound history and as viable theology. Why, then, make these works available once more?

First of all, this series does not represent an effort to turn the clock back, to declare these books to be the norm to which we should conform, either in method or in content. Neither critical research nor constructive theology can be repristinated. Nevertheless, root problems in the historical-critical study of Jesus and of theological reflection are perennial. Moreover, advances are generally made by a critical dialogue with the inherited tradition, whether in the historical reconstruction of the life of Jesus or in theology as a whole. Such a dialogue cannot occur, however, if the tradition is allowed to fade into the mists or is available to students only in handbooks which perpetuate the judgments and clichés of the intervening generation. But a major obstacle is the fact that certain pivotal works have never been available to the present generation, for they were either long out of print or not translated at all. A central aim, then, in republishing certain "Lives of Jesus" is to encourage a fresh discovery of and a lively debate with this tradition so that our own work may be richer and more precise.

Titles were selected which have proven to be significant for ongoing issues in Gospel study and in the theological enterprise as a whole. H. S. Reimarus inaugurated the truly critical investigation of Jesus and so was an obvious choice. His *On the Intention of Jesus* was reissued by the American Theological Library Association in 1962, but has not really entered the discussion despite the fact that questions he raised have been opened again, especially by S. G. F. Brandon's *Jesus and the Zealots*. Our edition, moreover, includes also his previously untranslated discussion of the resurrection and part of D. F. Strauss's evaluation of Reimarus. That Strauss's *Life of Jesus* must be included was clear from the start. Our edition, using George Eliot's translation, will take account of Strauss's shifting views as well. Schleiermacher's *Life of Jesus* will be translated, partly because it is significant for the study of Schleiermacher himself and partly because he is the wellspring of repeated concern for the inner life of Jesus. One of the most influential expressions of this motif came from Wilhelm Herrmann's *The Communion of the Christian with God,* which, while technically not a life of Jesus, emphasizes more than any other work the religious significance of Jesus' inner life. In fresh form, this emphasis has been rejuvenated in the current work of Ernst Fuchs and Gerhard Ebeling who concentrate on Jesus' own faith. Herrmann, then, is a bridge between Schleiermacher and the present. In such a series, it was also deemed important to translate Strauss's critique of Schleiermacher, *The Christ of Faith and the Jesus of History*, for here important critical issues were exposed. Probably no book was more significant for twentieth-century study of Jesus than Johannes Weiss's *Jesus' Proclamation of the Kingdom of God,* for together with Albert Schweitzer, Weiss turned the entire course of Jesus-research and undermined the foundations of the prevailing

Protestant theology. From the American scene, two writers from the same faculty were included: Shailer Mathews's *Jesus on Social Institutions* and Shirley Jackson Case's *Jesus: A New Biography.* There can be no substantive dialogue with our own theological tradition which ignores these influential figures, though today they are scarcely read at all. Doubtless other works could have been included with justification; however, these will suffice to enliven the theological scene if read perceptively.

In each case, an editor was invited to provide an introductory essay and annotations to the text in order to assist the reader in seeing the book in perspective. The bibliography will aid further research, though in no case was there an attempt to be comprehensive. The aim is not to produce critical editions in the technical sense (which would require a massive apparatus), but a useable series of texts with guidance at essential points. Within these aims the several editors enjoyed considerable latitude in developing their contributions. The series will achieve its aim if it facilitates a rediscovery of an exciting and controversial history and so makes our own work more fruitful.

The present volume is translated and edited by Richard H. Hiers and D. Larrimore Holland, who collaborated on all phases of the book. The interests and competences of these scholars complement each other to produce a major work in the series.

Richard H. Hiers was educated at Yale (B.A., B.D., M.A., Ph.D. 1954-61), where he also served as an assistant in instruction. Since 1961 he has been on the faculty in the Department of Religion at the University of Florida. Articles in professional journals attest his continuing interest in problems of the eschatology of the Synoptic Gospels and of Jesus. Two books explore related themes: *Jesus and*

Ethics (Westminster, 1968) and *The Kingdom of God in the Synoptic Tradition* (University of Florida Press, 1970), as well as a work in progress, *The Historical, Eschatological Jesus.*

D. Larrimore Holland earned his B.A. at DePauw (1955) and after a year at Tübingen as Fulbright scholar, earned the B.D., M.A. and Ph.D. at Yale (1959-62). For two years thereafter he taught church history and history of Christian thought at the Graduate School of Religion at the University of Southern California; subsequently he joined the faculty at McCormick Theological Seminary, where he is now Professor of Church History. In addition to his concentration on early church history and thought, he has maintained an interest in biblical studies, including field archeological experience at Shechem in 1966. A member of the editorial board of *Church History,* he has published widely in various professional journals and is at work on a major study of the early history of the Apostles' Creed.

LEANDER E. KECK

FOREWORD

Rudolf Bultmann[*]

Johannes Weiss (1863–1914) is characterized in the second edition of *Die Religion in Geschichte und Gegenwart* as "one of the founders of the eschatological movement in critical theology." In fact, his book *Die Predigt Jesu vom Reiche Gottes* . . . established his reputation. Here a consistent and comprehensive understanding of the eschatological character of the person and proclamation of Jesus was achieved and the course of further research definitively indicated. . . . At that time even Weiss himself could not have appreciated the importance of his findings.

Today the eschatological meaning of the preaching of Jesus, indeed, of the earliest Christian preaching generally, has become self-evident, and systematic theology draws the consequences from this recognition. Then, however, it came as a shock to the theological world. I still recall how Julius Kaftan in his lectures on dogmatics said, "If the Kingdom of God is an eschatological matter, then it is a useless concept so far as dogmatics is concerned." But despite numerous rejoinders and attempts to distort it, Johannes Weiss's judgment on the matter has prevailed triumphantly.

Most jolting were the consequences of the new insight for the understanding of Jesus' ethical instruction: The negative character of his crucial demands, the "interim"-

[*] Originally published in *Theologische Blätter* 18 (1939), pp. 242–246, and republished as a foreword to *Predigt*[3] (1964). Reproduced here in English translation by permission of Vandenhoeck & Ruprecht.

character of his ethics. How all this has worked itself out cannot be traced here. But one does well indeed to remember that the work once done by Johannes Weiss, Hermann Gunkel, Wilhelm Bousset, Wilhelm Heitmüller and their colleagues, precisely because it pushed the ideas of the New Testament back into the past, and because over against a middle class conception of Christianity it brought the strangeness of the New Testament startlingly to light, assisted in bringing forth a new and authentic understanding of the New Testament proclamation which at present is working itself out in all areas of theology. And for precisely that reason, Johannes Weiss's *Predigt Jesu* in particular has been of special importance.

INTRODUCTION

Richard H. Hiers and David Larrimore Holland

BIOGRAPHICAL NOTE

Johannes Weiss was born in Kiel, Germany, on December 13, 1863. He was the son of Bernhard Weiss, the noted New Testament scholar, commentator and textual critic. Johannes Weiss's education was at the Universities of Marburg, Berlin, Göttingen and Breslau between 1882-1888. As a *licentiatus theologiae,* he became a *Privatdozent* for New Testament in the University of Göttingen in 1888. Two years later he became an associate professor (*ausserordentlicher Professor*) of New Testament at the same university. Weiss accepted a call to become Professor (*ordentlicher Professor*) for New Testament at the University of Marburg in 1895, and three years later he moved to the University of Heidelberg where he remained until his sudden death at the age of fifty-one on August 14, 1914. His scholarly work encompassed not only his New Testament specialties, but also a rather wide range of social and religious interests.[1] He is generally associated with the socalled History of Religions School (*Religionsgeschichtliche Schule*) of German scholarship, though it is clear that his father's rather conservative perspective was not altogether obliterated from his outlook; likewise, his attitudes toward the German theologian, Albrecht Ritschl,[2] distinguished him from others of that school of thought. When he died,

1. See Bibliography for a partial listing.
2. See below, pp. 5–12, 15 ff.

1

Weiss left his *Das Urchristentum (Earliest Christianity)*, one of his most important and majestic works, unfinished. It was completed by his friend and colleague, Rudolf Knopf. Weiss also left an important legacy of students whom he had trained; perhaps best known among them is Rudolf Bultmann.

THE SIGNIFICANCE OF WEISS'S *PREDIGT*

Johannes Weiss is a name familiar to English-reading students primarily in connection with his *Earliest Christianity*.[3] Some are also acquainted with his commentary on Mark, *Das älteste Evangelium*. Both of these substantial works are important in their own right. But although both are informed by and consonant with Weiss's interpretation of New Testament eschatology, neither contains a systematic presentation of his findings with respect to this basic question. And yet the work in which these findings appear, *Die Predigt Jesu vom Reiche Gottes* ([1]1892, [2]1900), strangely has been neglected by British and American New Testament critics and theologians.

It was this work, however, which marks the turning point from nineteenth to twentieth century New Testament research. Both the "demythologizing" controversy and the "new quest of the historical Jesus," which first came to the attention of most American readers only in the 1950s, are responses to the eschatological interpretation of Jesus and the early Christian community. The eschatological interpretation made it clear that Jesus was not a modern man, that many of his beliefs and ideas (and those of the early church as well) cannot be presented to modern

3. For citations of Weiss's major works, see Bibliography. A short resumé of Weiss's career and writings is given in F. C. Grant's "Preface to the Torchbook Edition" of *Earliest Christianity* (New York: Harper, 1959), 1:v–xi.

believers as articles of faith. The mythological elements—
so Rudolf Bultmann proposed[4]—must be interpreted in
categories intelligible and credible to modern men. Of
course, the choice of existentialist categories by Bultmann
and his school did not follow inevitably from Weiss's recognition of the gap between the eschatological beliefs of Jesus
and those of modern men. But it certainly was Bultmann's
intention to express thereby the "understanding of existence" contained in such "myths."

Recognition of the eschatological beliefs of Jesus—a
recognition that by no means took place immediately or
without resistance—also meant that the historical Jesus
could no longer be identified either with the modern Jesus
of the "liberal lives of Jesus" or with the traditional Jesus
of Christian piety. Whereas the "old" quest of the historical Jesus had been undertaken by liberal writers in the
hope of finding a Jesus who, like themselves, could be liber-
ated from traditional dogmas,[5] the "new" quest has been
pursued by more theologically oriented writers with the
hope of discovering a historical Jesus who is not altogether
uncongenial, and, if possible, somehow related to the
kerygmatic Christ.

4. His classic statement of 1941, "New Testament and Mythology," is
printed as the first essay in Hans Werner Bartsch, ed., *Kerygma and Myth*,
trans. R. H. Fuller (New York: Harper Torchbooks, 1961), pp. 1–44;
see also Rudolf Bultmann, *Jesus Christ and Mythology* (New York:
Scribner's, 1958).

5. The "old" quest was not without other dogmatic interests, however:
see Reinhard Slenczka, *Geschichtlichkeit und Personsein Jesu Christi*
(Göttingen: Vandenhoeck & Ruprecht, 1967). But Robinson misrepre-
sents the "old" quest when he claims that its intent was to present the
historical Jesus "as a proven divine fact": James M. Robinson, *A New
Quest of the Historical Jesus* (London: SCM, 1959), pp. 44, 76 f. Cf.
Paul W. Meyer, "The Problem of the Messianic Self-consciousness of
Jesus," *NT* 4 (1960): 131 ff. For a critique of Robinson and defense of
Ritschl in this connection, see Daniel L. Deegan, "Albrecht Ritschl on the
Historical Jesus," *SJT* 15 (1962): 133–50.

One might also recognize Weiss as one of the prophets of form criticism. He was certainly as aware that the synoptic tradition had a history prior to its literary fixation as were such contemporaries as Martin Kähler and Wilhelm Wrede: "Every narrative that has been preserved, every saying that has survived, is evidence of some particular interest on the part of the primitive church."[6] But his most important contribution remains his recognition of the eschatological beliefs of Jesus and the early church and especially his willingness, against the stream of then contemporary theology, to try to discover what Jesus really understood the Kingdom of God to mean. In order to appreciate both the theological impact and the critical substance of the book, it seems fitting to take up these two questions separately.

Its Theological Impact

The appearance of Johannes Weiss's *Die Predigt Jesu vom Reiche Gottes* in 1892 produced a major crisis in European Protestant liberal theology. Since the time of Schleiermacher, that theology had been growing accustomed to the idea that the Christian religion was concerned primarily with religious experience of which Jesus was the great teacher and exemplar. The Kingdom of God, about which Jesus had preached and taught, was understood to refer ultimately to this experience. Wilhelm Herrmann and Adolf von Harnack, for example, understood it to mean the rule of God in the hearts of men. In circles more influenced by Immanuel Kant and Albrecht Ritschl, such as those of Julius Kaftan in Germany and the so-called Social Gospel movement as represented by Walter Rauschen-

6. Weiss, *Earliest Christianity*, 1:12; see also *Predigt²*, pp. 36 ff., 176 ff.; and *Das älteste Evangelium* (Göttingen: Vandenhoeck & Ruprecht, 1903), pp. 1 ff., 120 ff.

busch in America, the Kingdom was construed to mean the exercise of the moral life in society. The Kingdom of God was thought to be both immanent in individual religious experience and to be realized gradually in an ideal society on earth.

In less than sixty-seven pages, Weiss demonstrated that Jesus did not regard the Kingdom of God as a religious experience.

> The Kingdom of God as Jesus thought of it is never something subjective, inward, or spiritual, but is always the objective messianic Kingdom, which usually is pictured as a territory into which one enters, or as a land in which one has a share, or as a treasure which comes down from heaven.[7]

Weiss thereby also prevented his contemporaries from continuing to identify their idea of the Kingdom as supreme ethical ideal with what Jesus meant by it.

In setting forth the results of his research, Weiss raised two major questions. His primary concern was with the *historical* question: What does the New Testament reveal *Jesus* to have thought and taught about the Kingdom of God? But at the same time a second, essentially theological question also emerged: What is and what ought to be the relationship between Jesus' notion of the Kingdom and that of his disciples and of the church subsequently? In other words, Weiss was able to keep the historical and theological questions radically distinct in his own mind, and for that reason, so must we in our treatment of them here.

To turn to the first of the problems: Weiss was prodded into print by the growing tension between his own New Testament studies and the views of Ritschl (his father-in-law as well as his teacher) and the other liberal theologians

7. See below, p. 133.

(especially those influenced by Kant and the theology of the Enlightenment)[8] which he and his generation of students had imbibed. No doubt filial respect caused him to delay publication of his views until 1892, three years after the death of Ritschl, but by then he felt it necessary to make his findings public. As he writes in the foreword to his second edition of the *Predigt,*

> ... the clear perception that Ritschl's idea of the Kingdom of God and the corresponding idea in the proclamation of Jesus were two very different things disturbed me quite early. My publication of 1892 was an attempt to stress this difference sharply and vigorously. . . . The modern theological assertion is of a completely different form and mood from that of the earliest Christian notion.[9]

8. Weiss's *Die Idee des Reiches Gottes in der Theologie* (Giessen: J. Ricker'sche, 1901) contains a succinct and more explicit statement than *Predigt[1]* of Weiss's conviction that Ritschl's views were derived from the Enlightenment. (N.B.: Throughout the editor's introduction, *Predigt[1,2,3]* will be used for the first through the third editions respectively of *Die Predigt Jesu vom Reiche Gottes.* The third edition was edited by Ferdinand Hahn with a foreword by Rudolf Bultmann and published in Göttingen by Vandenhoeck & Ruprecht in 1964; except for Hahn's introduction and a different pagination for the preface by Weiss, the text in the third edition is identical with that of the second, which was published by Vandenhoeck & Ruprecht, 1900.)

9. *Predigt[2],* p. v. (= *Predigt[3],* p. xi.) Though the main thrust of J. Weiss's historical-critical study was directed against the kind of liberal theological position represented by his father-in-law, A. Ritschl, there was also a tacit repudiation of the more conservative theology of his father, Bernhard Weiss. The latter's *Life of Jesus,* published in 1882, trans. J. W. Hope (Edinburgh: T. & T. Clark, 1883–84), had been written as if there were no significant differences between the historical Jesus of the synoptic Gospels and traditional Christian affirmations about him. Accordingly, the elder Weiss did not bring the question of Jesus' eschatological beliefs into focus. B. Weiss was still living when *Die Predigt* was published, and his son pays him due respect (e.g., infra, pp. 61, 124). But the implications of J. Weiss's position pointed not only to the end of the era of liberal theology, but also placed in serious doubt the conservative equation of the historical Jesus with the Christ of traditional or "Biblical" piety.

When Weiss turned from current theology to the New Testament evidence, which he viewed through the eyes of the best critical scholarship of his time, he saw Jesus proclaiming a Kingdom of God which was unfamiliar. Ritschl's putative identification of his own view of the Kingdom with that of Jesus seemed false to Weiss. Whatever theological verdict one might render on Ritschl's notion of the Kingdom, one dared not, one *could* not—at least not on the New Testament's witness—confuse that view with what Jesus had thought and taught. Hence the first edition of the *Predigt* was at once a positive statement of the results of Weiss's New Testament research and a protest against what he regarded to be Ritschl's misunderstandings. Much of the form of Weiss's statement is controlled by this negative impulse. As a historian, he was determined to spike the weapons in the liberal arsenal. Therefore he set out not only to describe Jesus' views of the Kingdom of God accurately, but also to disarm the positions espoused by Ritschl and his followers and to defuse each of the exegetical arguments they had adapted to fortify their case.

The Eschatological Kingdom vs. the Ritschlian

The Kingdom of God which Weiss found on Jesus' lips in the New Testament had very different characteristics from that of Ritschl.[10] Ritschl had said,

> Those who believe in Christ are the Kingdom of God insofar as they, without reckoning the differences of sex, condition or nationality against each other, act reciprocally out of love and so bring forth on all possible levels and to the ends of the

10. On the whole question of the role of Weiss in the breakup of this sort of liberal theology, see. D. L. Holland, "History, Theology and the Kingdom of God: A Contribution of Johannes Weiss to Twentieth Century Theology," *Biblical Research* 13 (1968): 54–66.

7

human race the expanding community of moral conviction and moral goods.[11]

The sort of Kingdom of God Weiss traced to Jesus, however, was first of all "a *religious,* and in this case that means an *eschatological,* event."[12] The Kingdom was not primarily an ethical relationship of love for God and man. Moreover, the eschatology in which Jesus had framed his concept of the Kingdom was apocalyptic eschatology, which gave his proclamation a "religio-forensic character"[13] and severed its customary connections with the ethical idealism of nineteenth century liberal theology as Weiss knew it. The whole Ritschlian concept was out of kilter from this point of view.

Weiss traced the source of Jesus' notion of the Kingdom of God primarily to so-called late Jewish apocalypticism. In that thought-milieu, there was a dualism of worlds, one above and one here below. What happens here simply mirrors what has already happened decisively above.[14] One of the consequences of this line of thought is that a sharp dualism appears not only between the world above and this world below, but also between the rule of God and the rule of Satan.[15] Both sorts of dualism stand in conscious rebuke to the Ritschlian identification with Jesus' of its own monistic views of the Kingdom as a situation to be worked out here on earth among men. Weiss employs this sort of apocalyptic framework as his major touchstone of authenticity for distinguishing that which is genuinely attributable to Jesus in the New Testament from that which is plausibly the creation of the faith of the early church, a methodology

11. Albrecht Ritschl, *Die christliche Lehre von der Rechtfertigung und Versöhnung*[4] (Bonn: Marcus, 1895), vol. 3, p. 271.
12. *Predigt*[2], p. 146; cf. *Predigt*[1], below, pp. 82, 113–115, 132–135.
13. *Predigt*[2], p. 146.
14. See below, pp. 74–79.
15. See below, pp. 74–81, and cf. *Predigt*[2], pp. 29 ff.

which made the reproof of Ritschlian exegesis still more pronounced.[16]

Consequently, Weiss finds a number of characteristically apocalyptic and eschatological elements in Jesus' view of the Kingdom. Important among them is the radical transcendence of the Kingdom of God.[17] It is supramundane: "this old world cannot assimilate the Kingdom of God, the αἰὼν μέλλων; it must become new."[18] Whether conceived in terms of individual or collective morality or in terms of civic or ecclesiastical life, the Kingdom is not susceptible of being transposed into the world. Jesus, says Weiss, awaited a new heaven and a new earth. Secondly, the Kingdom of God was a matter for the future, not the present. "He (Jesus) has nothing in common with this world; he stands with one foot already in the future world."[19] To the question of whether Jesus expected the end to come immediately or whether he thought in terms of its being delayed until some time further off, Weiss finds a double answer in the New Testament. At first, he suggests, it is clear that Jesus expected the end imminently. All things were to come to their culmination shortly with the resurrection, the judgment, the millenial reign, and so forth.[20] But later in his life, Jesus' outlook on this matter shifted. He had been preaching a call to repentance, but the people had not repented. He then came to the conviction that the Kingdom would not come before his death and even that his own death would have a part in making it possible: his death would be a ransom for the people who were not responding

16. Cf. Christian Walther, *Typen des Reich-Gottes-Verständnisses* (Munich: Kaiser, 1961), pp. 161 f., for further discussion of this matter.
17. *Predigt²*, pp. 77 ff.
18. See below, pp. 93 ff.
19. *Predigt²*, p. 145. Cf. *Predigt¹*, see below, pp. 84–92.
20. See below, pp. 86 f., 129–131.

to his call to repent.[21] The end was still to come soon, but not before his own death had paved the way for it. Thirdly, the Kingdom was not to develop gradually from a small beginning. To think that was to grasp Jesus' meaning inadequately. "Either the Kingdom is here or it is not yet here!"[22] And, fourthly, it was not Jesus' mission—or even his view of his mission—to found or inaugurate the Kingdom. For every man, and that includes Jesus, the only viable attitude to take vis-à-vis the advent of the Kingdom was one of passivity. Men could pray that the Kingdom might come, but they could do nothing to bring it into existence. That remained forever solely the prerogative of God. The Kingdom was a gift, not an assignment.[23]

The ethic which one automatically expects to emerge from this view of the coming Kingdom will be negative and lean toward asceticism. The orientation will be away from this world and toward the future world. And such is what Weiss marks out in Jesus' teachings. Perhaps the ethic of Jesus, as Weiss details it, is most appropriately labeled a "penitential ethic."[24] It is not a positive ideal of worldly morality, such as Ritschl and his followers were disposed to elaborate, but the diametric opposite.[25] Every man is, however, enjoined to live so as to be prepared for the com-

21. See below, pp. 84–89.
22. See below, pp. 73 f. Cf. pp. 74 ff., and *Predigt²*, pp. 82 ff.
23. Liberal theology regarded it mainly as assignment: through moral effort, men were to build the Kingdom on earth. Adolf von Harnack thought that Jesus proclaimed the Kingdom as both gift and task (*What Is Christianity?* trans. T. B. Saunders [New York: Harper Torchbooks, 1957], p. 67).
24. Albert Schweitzer, in *The Quest of the Historical Jesus*, trans. W. Montgomery (New York: Macmillan, 1950), writes as follows: Weiss's "ethic is . . . completely negative . . . (in) character; it is, in fact, not so much an ethic as a penitential discipline" (p. 240). Both Weiss and Schweitzer understand Jesus to mean that only those who gave up all worldly ties and treasures would be fit to enter the Kingdom.
25. Cf., esp., *Predigt²*, pp. 145 ff.

ing Kingdom.[26] The end is upon us! Repent and get yourselves ready to enter the Kingdom! That is the crucial message. You yourselves can do nothing to effect the coming of
the Kingdom of God. God will see to that himself in his
own good time. But its appearance is close at hand, and you
can prepare yourselves so as to be ready when it comes.
"Jesus proclaimed what God desired of those who wished
in the future to participate in the Kingdom of God. The
new morality which he proclaimed was thought of as a condition for entrance into the Kingdom of God."[27] Thus, as
Weiss reads Jesus' teachings, the role of the Kingdom in
ethics is very different from Ritschl's assessment. It is no
longer the goal man strives to realize in his ethical life. It is
rather the motive for one's ethical life; one acts in such and
such a way because of the impending advent of the Kingdom. Ethics almost constitutes a sort of self-preparation of
a psychological sort, as Folke Holmström suggests.[28] Any
theory of rewards and punishments relating the notion of
the Kingdom of God and ethics, however, Weiss rejects
out of hand. The Kingdom itself is *eitel Gnade* (nothing
but grace)![29]

It should be noted, further, that there is a specific denial
in Weiss's study of any attempt to identify the Kingdom
with Jesus' circle of disciples. Idealistic theology in many
of its forms had too readily granted that identification, but

26. See below, pp. 105 ff.; cf. *Predigt*[2], pp. 95 f., 123–125, 157, 160.
27. *Predigt*[2], p. 138; cf. p. 126. Cf. also *Predigt*[1], below, pp. 105 ff., 132–
134.
28. Folke Holmström, *Det eskatologiska motivet i nutida teologi* (Stock-
holm: Svenska Kyrkans Diakonistyrelses, 1933), pp. 63–73, esp. p. 71;
an abridged German translation of this work appeared under the title
Das eschatologische Denken der Gegenwart, trans. Harold Kruska (Güters-
loh: C. Bertelsmann, 1936), p. 69; cf. also below, pp. 103 ff., and
Predigt[2], pp. 138 f., 150 f.
29. *Predigt*[2], p. 74; cf. pp. 76 f.

Weiss is explicit in his argument that the Kingdom of God does not consist in the disciples' recognition of the lordship of God in Jesus.[30] This argument is a good illustration of the way in which Weiss's exposition was controlled by his desire to rebuff the interpretation of the Ritschlians. There is, of course, a certain innate plausibility in Weiss's treating the question of the relationship of the disciples to the Kingdom, but there is certainly no necessity for his having raised the question with just this facet highlighted. One can conceive of his not having raised the question in this form at all save for the fact that this was the way liberal German theology was discussing this portion of the whole complex of problems surrounding the notion of the Kingdom of God.

Weiss thus found Jesus teaching about the Kingdom of God in purely eschatological terms. It was properly anticipated as an event to be brought about solely by the agency of God in the near future. One needed to prepare himself for its advent—that was the meaning of the preaching of Jesus—but one could then only wait passively for its coming.

In working out his eschatological interpretation of the New Testament data, Weiss encountered a major difficulty: certain dominical sayings which give every appearance of regarding the Kingdom as *present*. In *Predigt¹*, for instance, he is forced to treat Luke 17:21 (". . . for behold, the kingdom of God is in the midst of you") as the result of "prophetic enthusiasm"[31] and to relegate the "presence" sayings in general to a paradoxical manner of speaking[32] or to "expressions of spiritual ecstasy."[33] As he writes in

30. See below, pp. 68 ff., 129; *Predigt²*, pp. 78–88.
31. See below, pp. 78 f.
32. See below, pp. 72–75; cf. *Predigt²*, p. 87.
33. *Predigt²*, p. 90. Cf. the discussion in general in *Predigt¹*, below, pp. 65–81, and in *Predigt²*, pp. 65–99.

Predigt², ". . . it is only an intensification of his general certainty if now and then in joyful prophetic enthusiasm Jesus leaps across the short span of expectancy and speaks as if he were already at the goal."[34]

There is also a sense in which Jesus, according to Weiss, was aware that the forces of Satan had been broken in the world above and that, though he himself was still engaged in the battle here below, particularly in his exorcistic actions, the victory against the forces of Satan is in some meaningful way already assured.[35] To observe this also helps to explain Jesus' occasional proleptic utterances about the Kingdom's presence. Thus Weiss's final conclusion respecting the problems raised by these sayings is that they represent not so much shifts in Jesus' understanding as nuances of mood.[36] Basically these exceptional statements do not alter the judgment that Jesus' role in respect to the coming Kingdom is one of preparing the people for its future incursion, not one of presiding over its inauguration or development.

A related problem lies in what Weiss describes as a dichotomy between Jesus' views of the Kingdom and those of the earliest church as they are attested in the New Testament. It is an interesting feature of Weiss's whole enterprise in the two editions of the *Predigt* that he deals with this further question: Should Jesus' conception of the Kingdom be normative for subsequent Christian understanding? This question constitutes the second of the concerns mentioned above (p. 5).

Weiss discovered that even Jesus' disciples' idea of the Kingdom of God differed from Jesus': they weakened its eschatological character and brought it into the center of

34. *Predigt²,* p. 70.
35. See below, pp. 74–79.
36. *Predigt²,* pp. 70 f., 99.

13

their thought not as a future event but as something already present. Weiss found this quite comprehensible in view of the fact that these men, living as they did in the presence of Jesus, had a sense of the new order of things and the presence of the Kingdom in Jesus himself which obscured their perception of the eschatological kernel of Jesus' own understanding of the Kingdom. His interpretation of this phenomenon comes out perhaps most clearly in his treatment of Matt. 13:24 ff.[37] Weiss admits the evangelist understood his materials in terms of a present Kingdom but denies that the parable of the tares is really susceptible to that sort of exegesis. Such a rendering misses Jesus' message in the parable, and historical integrity demands we release it from the scheme in which the evangelist has enmeshed it. Thus Weiss exposes an important hiatus between the proclamations of Jesus and the early church.

Before we go on to the question of the perpetuation of that hiatus in modern theology and Weiss's comments upon it, a word or two is in order respecting the adequacy of Weiss's eschatological criterion for the authenticity of the tradition attributed to Jesus. Rolf Schäfer has restated an important kind of criticism of this facet of Weiss's work.[38] He suggests that the very standard Weiss employs to distinguish Jesus' words from those created by the faith of the church is artificial. For Schäfer, to use the thought-world of apocalypticism as the keystone for Jesus' genuine teachings is to take something foreign to the synoptic materials by which to judge them without first seeing what it is they can tell us. He sees a methodological contradiction in Weiss's work at this point. When one is trying consciously to rule out the views of the later church and to recapture

37. See below, pp. 61 f., 72; cf. *Predigt²*, pp. 40, 48.
38. Rolf Schäfer, "Das Reich Gottes bei Albrecht Ritschl und Johannes Weiss," *ZThK* 61 (1964): 68–88.

the pristine teaching of Jesus, he suggests, it is inappropriate to subordinate the ethical teachings ascribed to Jesus to the apocalyptic material.[39] This is especially the case when Weiss uses later materials—Pauline passages, sections from John, and even portions from the Revelation—to embellish and corroborate his points.[40] Furthermore, he thinks, this criterion causes Weiss to impute an apocalyptic sense to words which would not automatically incur such a meaning. And, more important still, it forces him to be a sort of Marcionite with respect to those portions of the text which do not readily support his theory; either such texts must be "corrected" to fit his view, or they must be eliminated for one reason or another. In other words, the major charge against Weiss's apocalyptic eschatology as a standard of authenticity is that it amounts to a *petitio principii*.

In a certain sense, of course, such a charge can scarcely be wholly denied, but the point is overstated. That Weiss sought to interpret the synoptic evidence with the help of other contemporary sources where similar or related apocalyptic concepts appear is certainly a less dubious procedure than that which was customary in his time, viz., to ignore the apocalyptic character of the New Testament materials. Moreover, in the academic and theological context in which the *Predigt* appeared, Weiss had to put his case as strongly as possible. If he overemphasized the eschatological aspects of the parables of the sower, the mustard seed, the leaven, the tares and the seeds growing secretly, it was clearly in order to counter the opposite interpretation at the hands of the Ritschlians.[41] If he denied interpretations which described the growth and expansion and development of the Kingdom when he treated these parables, it was

39. Ibid., pp. 73 ff.
40. See below, pp. 74 f., 92 f., 127.
41. See below, pp. 63 f., 70–74; cf. *Predigt*², pp. 82 ff.

primarily to win a hearing for certain data and for an interpretive option which were being totally neglected. Perhaps it would be fairer to Weiss to suggest that his criterion constitutes an exaggerated exegetical emphasis rather than a *petitio principii*. To be sure, Weiss also believed his interpretations to be essentially correct as well as an essential corrective for liberal theology's misconceptions—the vigor with which he defended his work against his critics in *Predigt*[2] attests to that—but the taut form in which he couched his first statement is rendered comprehensible and excusable in terms of the historical situation in which he wrote.

Ritschlian Theology, Nevertheless

We can now return to the question of the relationship between Jesus' proclamation of the Kingdom of God and the church's. Weiss, in recognizing that the earliest church had not followed Jesus' lead, that even among the disciples there had apparently been no ability to appropriate Jesus' idea without modification and mutation, also articulated an issue which went beyond the historical questions of Jesus' eschatology, namely, the question of the relation of the results of historical scholarship and contemporary theology. That is, he raises the question of hermeneutics. The timeliness of that question for today scarcely needs to be labored. Weiss as a historian and a theologian tried earnestly and honestly to ask how historical results coalesce with and impinge upon modern forms of the faith. He wanted to do both the historical and the contemporary theological tasks as well as possible, and, on the question of their relationship, he would allow the chips to fall where they might. He especially wanted to let the historical data speak for themselves, even if that eventuated in a break between New Testament exegesis and contemporary systematic theology.

As he examined both the New Testament and contemporary theology, he discovered a continuing hiatus between Jesus' and the church's thought on the Kingdom. That he regarded this gap as continuing down into the present from the earliest church is plain in his treatment of the position of Julius Wellhausen in *Predigt²*.[42] Weiss singled Wellhausen out as one who saw the Kingdom of God through Goethian glasses. He is quite complimentary of Wellhausen's treatment of the suprahistorical meaning of the Kingdom, but then goes on to say that "Wellhausen succumbs here to an old and widespread theological tradition which goes back finally to the Gospel of John," namely, the immanent and ethical interpretation of the Kingdom.[43] That is to say, Weiss does not treat Wellhausen's view as a uniquely modern malady, but sees it rather as yet another example of the de-eschatologizing which is already evident in the New Testament tradition.[44]

The basis for Weiss's attitude is clearly presented in his work *Die Idee des Reiches Gottes in der Theologie* (The Idea of the Kingdom of God in Theology), where he writes as follows:

> But however modernizing and dogmatizing Ritschl's biblical-theological foundation may be, the idea of the Kingdom of God as he formulates it need not therefore be unusable. For history shows that the idea of Jesus, except in the most ancient period, is never used in unabridged and undistorted form, but is always transposed and reinterpreted. It was simply impossible to use it otherwise. And if it is only useful and

42. Julius Wellhausen, „Des Menschen Sohn," in *Skizzen und Vorarbeiten*, sechstes Heft (Berlin: Georg Reimer, 1899), pp. 187–215. Weiss treats this point in *Predigt²*, pp. 55–65. It is worth noting, however, that Weiss did not really trace this issue in all its ramifications through the history of Christian theology.

43. *Predigt²*, p. 60.

44. Cf., esp., *Predigt²*, pp. 60–64.

pertinent in another form, then a use which deviates from the Bible appears to *me* at least inoffensive—especially if one is clear about the difference and regards it as essential.[45]

That is, Weiss regarded the historical and theological questions as separable. Historically speaking, Jesus' view of the Kingdom was eschatological but that of the church in Weiss's day was not, certainly not in the sense that Jesus' had been. But the theological evaluation of that discrepancy was a separate matter. Weiss was certainly neither a proto-"fundamentalist" nor one whose call was simply "back to the Bible!" He did not deny modern thought its viability. But he wanted to be sure his peers fully recognized that modern thought is not identical with Jesus' thought and expressions.

To make his position even clearer, Weiss was willing to ask if "Kingdom of God" was an appropriate designation for the modern concept, differing as it does from Jesus' use of the term.

> Jesus' idea of the Kingdom of God appears to be inextricably involved with a number of eschatological-apocalyptic views which systematic theology has been accustomed to take over without critical examination. But it is now necessary to ask whether it is really possible for theology to employ the idea of the Kingdom of God for the purpose for which it has recently been considered serviceable. The question arises whether it is not thereby divested of its essential traits and, in fact, so modified that only the name still remains the same.[46]

The position Weiss himself wants to embrace can be traced in his various works. When one compares the two

45. Weiss, *Idee des Reiches Gottes,* p. 113.
46. See below, p. 131; cf. pp. 134 f.; cf. Johannes Weiss, *Die Nachfolge Christi und die Predigt der Gegenwart* (Göttingen: Vandenhoeck & Ruprecht, 1895), p. 168 (hereafter cited as *Nachfolge*).

editions of the *Predigt,* it is clear that his historical position remained the same. In the eight years that lay between his two statements, he seems to have modified his views only in two respects: first, he could be somewhat less relentless in the exposition of his argument and the absoluteness of his terminology (as we shall see later); second, the later edition shows some traces of Weiss's own theological affinity for precisely the same Ritschlian position whose historical assumptions he so vigorously rejected. It is this latter element which introduces a certain diffuseness in Weiss's statement in the second, expanded edition. By the time of *Predigt²,* there appears to be a certain minoration of the eschatological outlook of the first edition. This alteration appears less as a change of mind or the result of new research than as a difference in the language chosen to expound the same historical materials.

This ambiguity becomes especially clear in the context of Weiss's other post-1892 writings which handle the same questions. *Die Nachfolge Christi und die Predigt der Gegenwart* (The Imitation of Christ and Contemporary Preaching)[47] for example, appeared in 1895 and was a clear declaration by Weiss that whatever the results of his historical research, the theological position demanded by the present was that approximated by liberal theology. One sees this position also emerging in a long article Weiss contributed to the *Archiv für Religionswissenschaft* entitled "Das Problem der Entstehung des Christentums" (The Problem of the Origin of Christianity).[48] There he writes as follows:

> For whoever already experiences the help and grace of God in the present life and has learned to rely on them has by that fact in principle overcome metaphysical dualism and

47. Ibid.
48. Weiss, *Archiv für Religionswissenschaft* 16 (1913): 423–515.

19

the tension toward the future. Now we observe this also in the proclamation of Jesus. Here the belief in God which, in itself, is completely uneschatological stands next to the eschatological frame of mind like something that can hardly be reconciled to it.[49]

The author of *Predigt¹* would scarcely have written those lines even though they do not necessarily contradict the historical position he was expounding there. Certainly the emphasis has shifted.

But Weiss the liberal Ritschlian theologian is apparent also in *Predigt²* (he had managed to remain largely hidden in *Predigt¹*). For example, in the second edition Weiss talked about the relation of the future and present sayings of Jesus concerning the Kingdom of God as nuances of mood, but in the first edition he found them rather more embarrassing exceptions to his stated position. Or, to take another example, the treatment of the commandment to love God and neighbor in *Predigt²* is handled as one of a series of noneschatological sayings which represent a different side of Jesus' teachings.[50] In this mood, Jesus repeated ethical dicta which were in common currency in his time and which reflect a more world-affirming tone than his own eschatological teachings. These noneschatological sayings, Weiss suggests, have a kind of abiding relevance which Jesus' own eschatological words by their very nature cannot have. (See the discussion below.)

What we have here labeled a diminution or minoration of the strict eschatology of *Predigt¹* by the time of *Predigt²* is, as suggested, less an intentional change on Weiss's part than a reflection—disallowed in the first edition, for the most part—of his own theology. He had made his point against the Ritschlians. Now his own questions as a son of

49. Ibid., p. 451.
50. *Predigt²*, pp. 134–138.

liberal theology could come to the fore with some sense of security against misunderstanding. Weiss was perfectly willing to accept the results of honest historical scholarship, whatever they might be. He was not prepared, however, to insist that the church in subsequent ages had to adhere to interpretations which were identical with those held by Jesus. He was ready to allow a radical hiatus to exist between Jesus' teachings and those of subsequent Christians. Indeed, he could see no alternative to that position. The plain meaning of the New Testament texts, as even the earliest Christian exegetes (e.g., Clement of Alexandria and Origen) had recognized, was utterly inapplicable in any literal sense to succeeding ages: Jesus' commandments were moral absolutes, but they were impossible to obey because they were inappropriate to changing situations. Weiss shared that judgment and notes, respecting Jesus' mandates, "It is self-evident that Jesus did not intend with them to promulgate for Christianity in all ages a continuing ethical law, an 'ordinance for the Kingdom of God'."[51] It had seemed to the church that those absolute commandments, therefore, had somehow either to be allegorized away or disposed of by some sort of exegetical exercise. And it was precisely those sorts of exegetical aberrations which Weiss rejected. The difficulty which had evoked them Weiss could appreciate, but as solutions they were unacceptable, for they attempted to confuse the historical and theological tasks by making their own findings seem to come from Jesus himself. "We must protest only against one who wants to eisegete this view, which was produced later, into the words and the faith of Jesus."[52] Historical integrity was required.

Nevertheless, after all the historical work was done,

51. *Predigt*[2], p. 143; cf. *Nachfolge*, p. 162.
52. *Predigt*[2], p. 177.

Weiss was still to maintain that the "modern" (sc. Ritschlian) notions of the Kingdom of God were the best for Christianity in his time. His point was simple, and it marked his views off from those of the other liberal theologians: Weiss did not need to have his own position seem to be identical with Jesus'. Weiss found, as did Schweitzer after him, that the historical Jesus, with his concern for an eschatological Kingdom, had almost nothing explicit to say respecting modern ethical issues. Consequently, if our modern notions of the Kingdom of God can help us with these issues, they, and not the views our historical research shows us Jesus held, are proper to us. This position comes to lucid expression all through Weiss's *Nachfolge;* there he says, for instance, "For these new questions, those words of Jesus give no directive however much one may want to apply them."[53] Further, "It can scarcely be imagined what a transformation of mood and ideas has taken place since it has become clear to mankind that they also have indeed to prepare this world as a place for the Kingdom of God, and that one is obliged to bequeath the coming generation a better world than one received."[54] The same view was incipiently present in *Predigt*[1]: "We no longer pray 'May grace come and the world pass away', but we pass our lives in the joyful certainty that this world will evermore become the showplace of a 'humanity of God'."[55] And this modern notion of the Kingdom could be described by Weiss as follows:

53. *Nachfolge,* p. 164.
54. *Nachfolge,* p. 163.
55. See below, p. 135. Cf. *Predigt*[2], p. v (= *Predigt*[3], p. xi): "I am still of the opinion today that his (Ritschl's) system and precisely this central idea represent that form of dogmatic statement which is best suited to draw our race to the Christian religion and, correctly understood and correctly expressed, to awaken and nurture a healthy and powerful religious life such as we need today."

We can trust permanently in the love of God with good conscience only if we desire with all our determination to be fellow-members of the community of the Kingdom of God, which, since Christ's work, is present within humanity, and if we are determined to cooperate with his wish in the strengthening and extension of the rule of God within ourselves and others and in his way to make the right, reverent, humble and faithful use of our position as children of our kingly Father.[56]

Neither historical research and modern theology nor the historical Jesus and the modern situation need be completely divorced, however. For even if Weiss refuses to relate them by means of what he considers bad exegesis so that modern versions—or perversions—of what Jesus is supposed to have taught are denied the authority of "as Jesus taught," he attempts another sort of reconciliation between Jesus and the present. If the eschatological words of Jesus give us no directive for our new questions, we can still rely upon the guidance of the exalted Christ. "Here again, our leader in (the social) struggle cannot be the historical Christ, but only the exalted Christ, of whom we believe that were he among us today, he would lead us in reorganizing the world according to the ideas which God reveals to us through history."[57] Just how that relationship with the exalted Christ is to come about and how it is to be described and what the relationship is between him and the historical Christ are matters Weiss does not clarify, but he relies explicitly and entirely on the veracity of Matt. 28:20b, "lo, I am with you always, to the close of the age." It would be wrong to imply, however, that we cannot have hints from the synoptic accounts of what we might find Jesus doing were he to reappear among us. His passionate

56. *Nachfolge*, p. 168.
57. *Nachfolge*, p. 164.

love for God and man and his earnest desire to bring all men to God would surely span the centuries. But we should not expect that he would simply repeat the Sermon on the Mount for us. Nor would he, in our circumstances, simply wait patiently for the coming of the Kingdom. He would set out to work for it in the framework of history. At one point Weiss goes so far as to claim of the historical Jesus that even "Had he not been drawn into the messianic movement through the call at the Jordan, possibly—in accord with his wholesome and luminous inmost nature—he would have become the founder of just as serious an 'evangelical' ethic, but one which delights in the world."[58] This, rather than a reproduction of Jesus' eschatological stance, is the sort of thing Weiss feels the world is now called upon by God to produce.

Subsequent Response

To review the subsequent discussions of the significance of eschatology for theology and ethics would require space beyond that allotted for this introduction. But a few words may be permitted.

Rudolf Bultmann has summarized the impact of Weiss's thesis upon the historical foundations of liberal theology:

> When I began to study theology, theologians as well as laymen were excited and frightened by the theories of Johannes Weiss. I remember that Julius Kaftan, my teacher in dogmatics in Berlin, said: "If Johannes Weiss is right and the conception of the kingdom of God is an eschatological one, then it is impossible to make use of this conception in dogmatics." But in the following years the theologians, J. Kaftan among them, became convinced that Weiss was correct.[59]

It is not surprising, then, that Bultmann describes Weiss's

58. *Predigt²*, p. 145.
59. Bultmann, *Jesus Christ and Mythology*, p. 13.

little book as "epoch-making."[60] Albert Schweitzer had earlier acclaimed it "one of the most important works in historical theology. It seems to break a spell. It closes one epoch and begins another."[61]

In the realm of moral theology, it needs scarcely be mentioned that the term "Kingdom of God" has now passed out of currency. Once the watchword of the Social Gospel movement, which looked for the establishment of the Kingdom—slowly, perhaps, but surely—on earth through human moral effort, this category has given place to others, for instance, in the terminology of Reinhold Niebuhr, to "prophetic religion." It is not the Kingdom of God, but, at best, "proximate solutions" which men strive to achieve on earth. Niebuhr's appreciation of the significance of the future *eschatological* fulfillment of the human situation appears in the second volume of his Gifford Lectures.[62]

The impact of the eschatological interpretation upon systematic theology has been somewhat less decisive. Prior to

---

60. Ibid., p. 12.

61. Schweitzer, *The Quest,* p. 239. It should be noted that this book, originally published in English in 1910, was translated from Schweitzer's *Von Reimarus zu Wrede* (Tübingen: Mohr [Siebeck], 1906). A revised and expanded edition was published in 1913 under the title, *Geschichte der Leben-Jesu-Forschung* (Tübingen: Mohr [Siebeck], 1913). The latter edition has been reprinted, but not, to date, translated. Schweitzer wrote a new foreword in 1950 for the 6th edition of *Geschichte* (Tübingen: Mohr [Siebeck], 1951) in which he restated and reaffirmed his basic viewpoint. This new foreword is translated by J. R. Coates—rather freely —in the 3rd English edition of *The Quest* (London: A. & C. Black, 1964). Schweitzer also reviewed his position with respect to Jesus' understanding of the Kingdom in another manuscript completed in 1951: *The Kingdom of God and Primitive Christianity* (New York: Seabury, 1968), pp. 68–130.

62. Reinhold Niebuhr, *The Nature and Destiny of Man* (New York: Scribner's, 1943), esp. pp. 244–300. Cf. Harvey Cox's hopeful effort to revive the Kingdom of God as a basic category for contemporary social ethics: *The Secular City* (New York: Macmillan, 1965), pp. 110–113, 124 ff.

the discovery of Jesus' (and early Christianity's) eschatological world-view, there was no need for a program of demythologizing. Eschatology had been demythologized, but for the most part, covertly and even subconsciously, not only, as we shall see, by the writers of the "lives of Jesus," but also by preachers and the writers of dogmatics. Eschatology was generally treated as meaning life after death, and the Kingdom of God was equated—if not with social progress and/or individual religious experience—with the church, especially the "dead in Christ" now in heaven. Rudolf Bultmann proposed to express the essential meaning of New Testament eschatology in existentialist categories. In the "now" or "crisis of decision," in response to the address or demand of the kerygma, one makes a decision of final consequence for his own future. This "now" of hearing and responding to the kerygma, in fact, constitutes the eschatological moment, linking one with the "eschatological event," Jesus Christ.[63] But in Bultmann's interpretation of eschatology, nearly everything is concentrated upon the present. If the link between the present eschatological moment and the past, the "Christ event," is tenuous and problematic (a point of concern to many of Bultmann's "pupils," e.g., E. Käsemann), the line to the future seems to be missing entirely. Bultmann believes that the virtual elimination of the future may be justified by pointing to the Fourth Gospel's proclivity toward "realized eschatology." Further to justify this procedure, Bultmann insists that the traces of a futuristic eschatology which ap-

63. See the discussions in the several volumes edited by Hans Werner Bartsch entitled *Kerygma and Mythos,* some of which have been translated by R. H. Fuller: *Kerygma and Myth,* 1, 2 (London: SPCK, 1953, 1962). For criticism of Bultmann's (and his followers') tendency to eliminate the significance of the Kingdom as future event, see Otto Betz, *What Do We Know About Jesus?* (Philadelphia: Westminster, 1968), pp. 45–47.

pear in John should be discounted as secondary interpolations! Karl Barth's interpretation of eschatology, like that of the Fourth Gospel, begins and all but ends with the incarnation. Bultmann is preoccupied with the present subjective moment of existential decision; Barth with the past and (to him) objective events from Jesus' incarnation through his ascension. Each interprets eschatology primarily in terms of his respective theological interest; neither takes chronological futurity seriously. Oscar Cullmann's *Christ and Time* presents another interpretation of the meaning of New Testament eschatology: Christ stands midway between the beginning and end of time and history —the end is yet to come as "final completion," but the "when" makes no difference, for "the 'end' as the meaning of redemptive history . . . is Jesus Christ, who has already appeared."[64] So far as dogmatics is concerned, the general tendency of these writers is toward realized eschatology. The same is true of most of the so-called post-Bultmannian writers, e.g., Günther Bornkamm, Hans Conzelmann, and James M. Robinson.

Various other eschatological doctrines appear which are less influenced by the eschatological interpretation of the New Testament. Dietrich Bonhoeffer and Teilhard de Chardin, both of whom have posthumously enjoyed considerable interest recently in America, thought in terms of an evolutionary or developmental teleology: respectively, toward a secular world "come of age," and toward increasing consciousness on the part of being. Tillich used the category "Kingdom of God" as a subtitle in volume 3 of his *Systematic Theology,* but wrote as if he had not yet heard of Weiss or Schweitzer. For Tillich, the Kingdom of God

64. Oscar Cullmann, *Christ and Time,* trans. F. V. Filson, rev. ed. (Philadelphia: Westminster, 1964), pp. 139–43.

meant basically "the transition from the temporal to the eternal."[65]

Recently, however, new efforts to express the significance of the eschatological future for theology have appeared, most notably, those of Jürgen Moltmann.[66] What place eschatology will have in future discussions of dogmatics remains to be seen. It is unlikely, however, that it will be tacitly demythologized or simply ignored.

The Consequences for New Testament Research

Die Predigt Jesu vom Reiche Gottes also opened a new era in New Testament research. When the eschatological beliefs of Jesus were taken seriously, it was no longer possible for modern interpreters to fashion the "historical Jesus" after their own images, as had been the custom among the nineteenth century writers of "lives of Jesus."[67] Now a more historically accurate account of his preaching, activity, and intention would have to be attempted. Hitherto, it had generally been supposed that Jesus did not really believe that the Kingdom of God or messianic age would soon appear. These topics had been subsumed under theological ethics. But now it was possible and, indeed, necessary to raise the more basic question: What religious meaning do these beliefs express? Bultmann's famous program of "demythologizing" is concerned with precisely this question. The new appreciation of eschatology also made possi-

65. Paul Tillich, *Systematic Theology*, 3 (Chicago: Univ. of Chicago Press, 1963), esp. pp. 394–423. D. M. Smith, Jr., observes that Tillich, in *Systematic Theology* 2, "utilizes C. H. Dodd's realized eschatology as the true understanding of Jesus' Kingdom proclamation": "The Historical Jesus in Paul Tillich's Christology," *JR* 46 (1966): 146.
66. Jürgen Moltmann, *Theology of Hope*, trans. J. W. Leitch (London: SCM; New York: Harper, 1967), and "Resurrection as Hope," *HTR* 61 (1968): 129–48. Also Paul S. Minear, *Christian Hope and the Second Coming* (Philadelphia: Westminster, 1954).
67. See Schweitzer, *The Quest*, esp. chs. xiv–xvi, xx.

ble a more accurate understanding of the beliefs and expectations of the early Christian community, which now could be characterized as the "eschatological congregation."[68]

Earlier Eschatological Theories

Weiss was not, however, the first to identify the eschatological character of Jesus' beliefs. He notes with appreciation the appearance in 1891 of the volumes by Otto Schmoller and Ernst Issel.[69] And Hermann Samuel Reimarus, in the eighteenth century, had proposed that Jesus and his disciples shared the eschatological beliefs of their contemporaries and had gone on to claim that Jesus understood his role as that of the *political* messiah who would lead his people in revolt against the Roman authorities and thereby establish the messianic Kingdom.[70] Though it is

---

68. E.g., Rudolf Bultmann, *Theology of the New Testament,* trans. Kendrick Grobel (New York: Scribner's, 1954), 1: 37 ff.

69. Otto Schmoller, *Die Lehre vom Reiche Gottes in den Schriften des Neuen Testaments* (Leiden: E. J. Brill, 1891), and Ernst Issel, *Die Lehre vom Reiche Gottes im Neuen Testament* (Leiden: E. J. Brill, 1891); Weiss commended both in his preface to *Predigt*[1]; see below, p. 56. Issel maintained that Jesus regarded himself as the "Founder" of the Kingdom of God, which was to be interpreted as "highest good" and "highest task" (p. 51); but insisted that Jesus also looked forward to the consummation of the Kingdom or its coming "in power" at the time of the Judgment. Schmoller's interpretation more closely approaches that of Johannes Weiss and Albert Schweitzer. He maintained that Jesus came as Messiah, but that his earthly ministry was preparatory; the Kingdom of God was as yet present only in heaven; it would first come to earth upon Jesus' return in the future (see esp., pp. 155–170). Schmoller also anticipated Weiss's and Schweitzer's interpretation of the relation of ethics and eschatology: Jesus proclaimed repentance as "a condition for admission into the Kingdom" (p. 44).

70. Hermann Samuel Reimarus, *Von dem Zwecke Jesu und seiner Jünger,* ed. G. E. Lessing (Berlin: Sander, 1778). This work has been published as *Reimarus: Fragments,* The Lives of Jesus (Philadelphia: Fortress, 1970). The interpretation of Jesus as a political messiah or revolutionary has recently been popularized in the writings of S. G. F. Brandon and H. J. Schonfield.

now generally agreed that Reimarus was mistaken in classifying Jesus mainly as a political and revolutionary messiah, Weiss was to follow him and recognize that Jesus' eschatological expectation did indeed contain radical political implications: when the Kingdom of God was established, the Roman authorities naturally would no longer rule. Jesus and the twelve disciples would then reign over the members of the Kingdom. But God himself, not human arms, would bring about this "revolution." Men could only wait and make themselves ready for this momentous event and era.[71] A few others such as D. F. Strauss, in his first *Life of Jesus* (1835), F. W. Ghillany, and Wilhelm Baldensperger, had partially grasped the eschatological character of Jesus' beliefs and ministry also, but none had set it forth as clearly and simply as did Weiss in 1892.

Weiss, Schweitzer and Consistent Eschatology

Weiss was soon joined by a formidable ally, Albert Schweitzer. The latter's *Skizze des Lebens Jesu* (Sketch of the Life of Jesus)[72] appeared a year after the publication of Weiss's revised and expanded edition of the *Predigt*. Apparently Schweitzer had not as yet read either edition of Weiss's work,[73] but many of his conclusions were similar to Weiss's. Schweitzer later believed in retrospect that he had gone further than Weiss. While Weiss had defined the es-

71. See below, pp. 102 f.; cf. *Predigt²*, pp. 121–125.
72. Albert Schweitzer, *Das Messianitäts- und Leidensgeheimnis. Eine Skizze des Lebens Jesu* (Tübingen: Mohr [Siebeck], 1901); trans. W. Lowrie, *The Mystery of the Kingdom of God* (London: A. & C. Black, 1925; New York: Macmillan, 1950).
73. Evidently Schweitzer's position was based on his own independent studies of the text beginning as early as 1894: see Albert Schweitzer, *Out of My Life and Thought,* trans. C. T. Campion (New York: Henry Holt & Co., 1933, 1949), pp. 6–8, 13 f. There is no mention of Weiss in Schweitzer's own "sketch" of the life of Jesus published in 1901.

chatological elements in Jesus' *preaching* accurately, he failed—in Schweitzer's judgment—to recognize the eschatological character of Jesus' *ministry*.

Schweitzer used the term *konsequente Eschatologie* ("consistent" or "thorough-going" eschatology) to differentiate his own theory that "the whole public work of Jesus" is to be explained by reference to his eschatological beliefs from Weiss's application of "the eschatological explanation only to the preaching of Jesus."[74]

> . . . (Weiss) comes to a stop halfway. He makes Jesus think and talk eschatologically without proceeding to the natural inference that His actions also must have been determined by eschatological ideas.[75]

Curiously, the precise meaning of *konsequente Eschatologie* has escaped most (but especially Anglo-Saxon) interpreters. Norman Perrin, for instance, supposes that Schweitzer applied the term to Weiss's interpretation as well as to his own.[76] C. H. Dodd thinks that *"consequente Eschatologie"* referred only to Jesus' sayings about the Kingdom. Some of the sayings, Dodd notes, apparently expressed the idea that the Kingdom was future, while others implied that it was present. In the face of this evidence, he suggests, *"consequente Eschatologie"* was de-

---

74. Schweitzer, *The Quest* (1950), pp. 350 f.; Schweitzer, *Geschichte,* pp. 390 f.

75. Schweitzer, *Out of My Life and Thought,* p. 48. Cf. *The Quest¹,* p. 351, n. 1.

76. Norman Perrin, *The Kingdom of God in the Teaching of Jesus* (Philadelphia: Westminster, 1963), p. 32, n. 1. Archibald M. Hunter declares that Weiss was a proponent of "consistent eschatology": *The Work and Words of Jesus* (Philadelphia: Westminster, 1950), p. 12. Cecil J. Cadoux makes the same mistake: *The Historic Mission of Jesus* (New York: Harper, n.d.), p. 129. So also George E. Ladd, *Jesus and the Kingdom* (New York: Harper, 1964), pp. 4 ff., 220; and C. C. McCown, "Jesus, Son of Man," *JR* 28 (1948): 2.

vised as a "compromise" which represented the Kingdom "as coming very, very soon."[77] This explanation of *konsequente Eschatologie* and its inception is, of course, totally erroneous.

Schweitzer, however, may have exaggerated the difference between *konsequente Eschatologie* and Weiss's theory. Weiss did interpret Jesus' thought and sayings eschatologically. But he also explained some of his actions accordingly. In fact, Weiss pays more attention than Schweitzer himself to Jesus' activity as exorcist. In these exorcisms, Weiss states, Jesus "is conscious of carrying on a struggle against the Satanic kingdom" whereby "he was taking ever vaster provinces of this kingdom away from the rule of the Prince of this world."[78] Weiss regards this activity of Jesus as preliminary to and preparatory for the coming of the Kingdom. Indeed, he suggests, if one wishes to speak of Jesus as the "Founder" of the Kingdom of God, one can do so legitimately only if one is prepared to think of the matter in terms of this mythological idea of his warfare against Satan's kingdom.[79]

Weiss also connects Jesus' decision to die in Jerusalem with his eschatological beliefs. He does not, to be sure, work out as precise a theory in this connection as Schweitzer does. The latter explained that Jesus was convinced that

---

77. C. H. Dodd, *The Parables of the Kingdom,* 2nd rev. ed. (New York: Scribner's, 1961), p. 34.

78. See below, pp. 76 f.; cf. *Predigt²,* pp. 91, 116 f.

79. See below, p. 80, where Weiss also writes, "He (Jesus) prepares the way for the Kingdom of God in that he is successfully engaged in driving the present ruler of this age, Satan, from his position of lordship." Strack-Billerbeck present evidence that first to fifth century Judaism took Satan and the demons quite seriously: 1, 136–144; 4, 501–535. So also Paul Volz, *Die Eschatologie der jüdischen Gemeinde,* 2nd ed. (Tübingen: Mohr [Siebeck], 1934), pp. 8, 68. Cf. also Samuel Sandmel, *The First Christian Century in Judaism and Christianity* (New York: Oxford, 1969), pp. 35 ff.

the final tribulation (ὁ πειρασμός) must be endured before the Kingdom could come. In Jerusalem, Jesus deliberately provoked the authorities into executing him so that he himself might suffer on behalf of "many," the elect, and thereby spare them the necessity of sharing that fate. At the same time he would be removing the final obstacle in the way of the Kingdom's appearance, namely, that to date the tribulation had not yet occurred. At points, however, Weiss does hint at some approximation of this theory. Instead of the tribulation, Weiss proposes that the sin or guilt of the people was the "obstacle" to be atoned for before the Kingdom could come. Jesus did not seek to die, but came to recognize that his enemies would kill him before the Kingdom could come. He realized then that his death would be the means whereby the obstacle of guilt was to be removed. His death, thus, would contribute to the establishment of the Kingdom.[80]

Elsewhere, however, Weiss states that Jesus understood that the Kingdom would not come until his followers, by their preaching, had succeeded in arousing the people to repentance. Again, Weiss states that Jesus regarded his death as a "sin offering" which would ransom the people from the otherwise inevitable death penalty. Nevertheless, they must repent or the "sin offering" will be forfeited and they will be abandoned to destruction at the time of judgment.[81] Once again, it is not clear how Weiss thought Jesus believed that his death would "contribute to the establishment of the Kingdom of God."[82] The "sin offering" of his

---

80. See below, pp. 86–89, 130; cf. also *Predigt²*, p. 103: "His death cannot signify the ruin of his work, but only a means for the establishment of the Kingdom of God."

81. See below, p. 100.

82. Nor does Weiss develop an explicit connection between Jesus' sacrificial death and the future coming of the Kingdom in his analysis of Mark 10:45 in *Predigt²*. Many interpreters since Weiss have hinted at

death would only be effective when the people had repented. It would, in any case, serve as a ransom for sinners,
making it possible for them to inherit the Kingdom, whenever it should come, providing only that they repent in the
final remaining moments of history. Weiss did not claim
that Jesus sought to die in Jerusalem, only that he believed
his death would somehow contribute to the coming of the
Kingdom. Schweitzer is partly, but not entirely, correct in
saying that Weiss applied the eschatological interpretation
only to Jesus' thought and teaching.

Subsequent Responses to Die Predigt and Eschatology

Strangely enough, although *Die Predigt Jesu vom Reiche
Gottes* aroused considerable response among European
writers,[83] it has had little impact on British and American
New Testament scholarship. B. W. Bacon, B. H. Brans-
comb, W. E. Bundy, E. C. Colwell, C. H. Dodd, A. M.
Hunter, T. W. Manson, and E. F. Scott make no mention
of it in their writings. The title appears in Amos Wilder's
Eschatology and Ethics in the Teaching of Jesus,[84] but only
in the bibliography. J. A. T. Robinson and John Knox refer
to it, once each, in footnotes,[85] but it does not figure in their

some such connection, but like Weiss, they generally leave their understanding vague: e.g., Oscar Cullmann, *Le Retour du Christ* (Neuchâtel,
Paris: Delachaux et Niestlé, 1944), pp. 26 f.; Joachim Jeremias, *The
Eucharistic Words of Jesus,* trans. A. Ehrhardt (Oxford: Basil Blackwell,
1955), pp. 148, 152; John A. T. Robinson, *Jesus and His Coming* (New
York: Abingdon, 1957), p. 81; Rudolf Schnackenburg, *God's Rule and
Kingdom,* trans. J. Murray (New York: Herder & Herder, 1963), pp. 250 ff.
83. E.g., Wilhelm Bousset, Paul Wernle, Julius Wellhausen; more recently, Rudolf Bultmann and W. G. Kümmel.
84. Amos Wilder, *Eschatology and Ethics in the Teaching of Jesus,* rev.
ed. (New York: Harper, 1950).
85. J. A. T. Robinson, *Jesus and His Coming* (New York: Abingdon,
1957), p. 13; John Knox, *Jesus, Lord and Christ* (New York: Harper,
1958), p. 85.

discussions of Jesus' eschatological beliefs. Nearly all of these writers refer to Schweitzer as if he were the inventor of the eschatological interpretation. Weiss's name does not appear among the references in the articles "Eschatology of the New Testament" and "Kingdom of God" in *Hastings' Dictionary of the Bible* (1898, 1899). The viewpoint here was still very largely controlled by the literature of A. Ritschl, H. J. Holtzmann, H. H. Wendt, with some reference also to B. Weiss. Two other articles, one by W. Adams Brown, the other by William Sanday,[86] list *Predigt¹* among recent monographs, but neither article appears to have been informed by a reading of the little book. Later, in *The Life of Jesus in Recent Research*,[87] fully half of which he acknowledges "as really based upon Schweitzer's labours,"[88] Sanday admits that he had "unfortunately missed the first edition [*Predigt¹*] when it came out" and had to base his sketch of Weiss's position "mainly on Schweitzer's summary" in *Von Reimarus zu Wrede*.[89] There is virtually no mention of Weiss's *Predigt,* or even of eschatology, in the *Journal of Biblical Literature* and the *American Journal of Theology* during the decade following 1892. The articles which mention the Kingdom of God treat it primarily as a spiritual entity founded by Jesus. For such American writers as Shailer Mathews and Benjamin W. Bacon, the leading authorities remained B. Weiss, H. H. Wendt, and W. Beyschlag. An article by Bacon in 1903, however, evidences Weiss's and/or Schweitzer's influence—though he

---

86. James Hastings, ed., *Dictionary of the Bible* (Edinburgh: T. & T. Clark), 4 (1902), pp. 362 ff.; 2 (1899), pp. 603 ff., respectively.
87. William Sanday, *The Life of Jesus in Recent Research* (New York: Oxford, 1908).
88. Ibid., p. 45.
89. Ibid., pp. 56–60. He notes that he could find no copy of *Predigt¹* in Oxford, but had, at last, in 1907, located the Cambridge Library copy!

mentions neither's name.[90] From the lack of attention it has been given, one receives the impression that the *Predigt* has been generally unknown in Britain and America, possibly, in part, because copies of it have been unavailable. (A recent notable exception is Norman Perrin, who devotes several pages to a review of Weiss's position.)[91] The fact that Weiss's book has not previously been translated may also be a factor.[92] In any case, the present publication of the *Predigt* in English should not be merely of antiquarian interest.

The great majority of European New Testament scholars, however, have accepted Weiss's and Schweitzer's conclusion that Jesus expected the Kingdom to come in the near future. Indeed, in 1956 Bultmann could write, "Today nobody doubts that Jesus' conception of the Kingdom of God is an eschatological one—at least in European theology . . . ."[93] On the other hand, especially since C. H. Dodd's exegetical efforts on behalf of so-called realized eschatology,[94] it has seemed to many interpreters, especially

90. Here Bacon affirms that Jesus shared the apocalyptic beliefs of his contemporaries and, indeed, emphasized the imminence of the Parousia, Judgment and Kingdom. Like Bultmann after him, Bacon viewed Jesus' fallibility with equanimity, for Christianity was not fashioned out of the story of Jesus, but upon it: upon the knowledge of Christ "according to the Spirit." Benjamin W. Bacon, "Ultimate Problems of Biblical Science," *JBL* 22 (1903): 7–14.

91. Perrin, *Kingdom of God,* pp. 16–23. He does not mention Weiss, however, in his more recent study, *Rediscovering the Teaching of Jesus* (New York: Harper, 1967), in which his predilection for "realized eschatology" is still more obvious. In his chapter on the Kingdom of God, he makes no reference to its future coming! For further criticism of Perrin's attempt to eliminate Jesus' futuristic expectation, see the reviews by W. G. Kümmel and J. B. Cobb, Jr., in *JR* 49 (1969): 61–65, 194 f.

92. Nearly every subsequent Anglo-Saxon writer refers to Schweitzer's *The Quest.*

93. Bultmann, *Jesus Christ and Mythology,* p. 13.

94. C. H. Dodd, *Parables of the Kingdom* (London: Nisbet & Co., 1935, rev. 1936 and 1961).

in Britain and America, that in some way or other Jesus also thought that the Kingdom was present. Dodd maintains that Jesus believed that the Kingdom of God was entirely present: there would be no future coming of the Kingdom of God, or, for that matter, of the Messiah (or Son of man) or Judgment. All these eschatological phenomena were already realized.[95] Few, if any, other New Testament scholars are willing to go quite so far.

The Relation of the Future Kingdom to "Realized Eschatology"

One of the central questions in New Testament study for the last several decades, therefore, has been this: How could Jesus have thought of the Kingdom as both present and future? Some of the synoptic evidence makes it clear that Jesus expected the Kingdom to come in the future. Other synoptic evidence lends support to "realized eschatology." How is this apparently contradictory evidence to be explained?

Weiss's position. Several of the hypotheses put forth since 1900 had appeared earlier in similar form and been rejected by Weiss. Among these was the proposal that Jesus visualized the arrival of the Kingdom in two stages or phases, sometimes designated respectively the "fulfillment of the Kingdom" and the "consummation" or "completion" of the Kingdom.[96] As Weiss countered, however, the

95. Some of Dodd's interpreters have claimed that he has retreated from "realized eschatology" in recent years (e.g., Perrin, *Kingdom of God,* p. 159). But Dodd's latest revision of *Parables of the Kingdom* (1961) reveals no change in his basic position.
96. Advocated more recently by Ladd, *Jesus and Kingdom,* pp. 101 ff.; Herman Ridderbos, *The Coming of the Kingdom,* trans. H. de Jongste, ed. R. O. Zorn (Nutley, N.J.: The Presbyterian & Reformed Publishing Co., 1962), pp. 47 ff., 56; but compare p. 105. Thus also Oscar Cullmann

synoptic evidence does not support such a distinction. Jesus did not teach his disciples to pray for the *completion* of the Kingdom, but for its *coming*.[97] The term συντέλεια (τοῦ) αἰῶνος ("consummation" or "close of the age") appears five times in Matthew, but in each case it is the consummation or close of the *present* age, not of the Kingdom of God. *Prophecies* are fulfilled (e.g., Luke 4:18–21); and the *time* is fulfilled (Mark 1:15); but Jesus is nowhere reported to have said that the *Kingdom* had been fulfilled.

Some interpreters[98] have urged that Mark 9:1 implies that Jesus believed that the Kingdom was already present, but hidden. Those standing here cannot see it; however, they will see it when it comes *with power* (ἐν δυνάμει). Against this line of interpretation, Weiss urges that the phrase is secondary.[99] In any event, the fact that the Kingdom was expected to come ἐν δυνάμει does not mean that it is already present. How else would the Kingdom of God come *but* with power, even violence and destruction, doing away with the old world or the present age in a dramatic and universally visible fashion?[100] When the Kingdom comes, it will be "with power" or "powerfully"; but that does not mean that it is now present without power—or even in any preliminary way at all.

---

and W. G. Kümmel. Perrin suggests a similar distinction between men's present "experience" of the Kingdom, and a future "consummation." *Rediscovering*, pp. 160 f.

97. Matt. 6:10. See below, p. 73. Perrin's exegesis of this petition is implausible: *Rediscovering*, pp. 160 f.

98. E.g., C. H. Dodd, T. W. Manson.

99. See below, p. 97, author's footnote.

100. The phrase "in power" is used elsewhere to characterize the way in which the Son of man will come: e.g., Mark 13:26 = Matt. 24:30 = Luke 21:27. Cf. Luke 17:22–37, and Weiss's comment: "The establishment of the Kingdom of God will not take place in a corner." When the Kingdom comes, the old world will be broken up and transformed. See below, pp. 92 f. and *Predigt²*, pp. 106 f.

A few scholars have urged that at least some of Jesus' sayings about the present Kingdom referred to the church, or at any rate, to the band of disciples that was gathering about him. This view is championed, for instance, by Ernst Troeltsch, T. W. Manson and, among other Roman Catholic writers, Karl Adam. Weiss, however, made it plain in 1892 that the equation of the Kingdom with Jesus' disciples or the church cannot be attributed to Jesus.[101]

Again, it has been asserted that Jesus thought that the Kingdom had already come in his own person or ministry.[102] The advocate of this theory generally leans heavily on Luke 17:20 f. (. . . he answered them, "The kingdom of God is not coming with signs to be observed; nor will they say, 'Lo, here it is!' or 'There!' for behold, the kingdom of God is in the midst of you.") That saying, however, can be so construed only arbitrarily, Weiss insists.[103] One might, he concedes, properly speak of Jesus as the "Founder" of the Kingdom, but not in the manner in which that term is ordinarily used.[104] But the Kingdom can hardly be identified with his person or ministry: Jesus' ministry is *preparatory*.[105]

101. See below, pp. 68–70, 83 f. Cf. the discussion above, pp. 11 f. Weiss continued to insist on this point in *Predigt²*, pp. 176 f. Schnackenburg, a recent Catholic writer, argues against this equation: *God's Rule*, pp. 232 f.

102. Thus, e.g., W. G. Kümmel, *Promise and Fulfillment,* trans. D. M. Barton, SBT no. 23, (London: SCM, 1957): 105 ff. C. K. Barrett, *The Holy Spirit and the Gospel Tradition* (London: SPCK, 1947), pp. 156–57; William Barclay, *The Mind of Jesus* (London: SCM, 1960), pp. 61–62; A. L. Moore, *The Parousia in the New Testament,* Supplements to *Novum Testamentum* 13 (Leiden: Brill, 1966), pp. 63, 104. H. Koester has recently proposed that Jesus proclaimed that the Kingdom was present in his words or message: "One Jesus and Four Primitive Gospels," *HTR* 61 (1968): 217 ff. But the best support Koester can find for his proposal is *Gospel of Thomas* 91!

103. See below, pp. 72 f., 89–91; cf. *Predigt²*, p. 86.

104. See below, pp. 79–81.

105. See below, pp. 76–80.

Others[106] have proposed that Jesus understood the Kingdom to be present; the future would bring the Last Judgment and Parousia or Final Consummation. In the meantime, man could enter the Kingdom of God. Against such a view, Weiss had already declared: "There can be no doubt that Jesus regarded (the) Judgment as prior to the establishment of the Kingdom."[107] His point is that the passages (e.g., Matt. 11:11; 21:31) which are supposed to show that there are some who have already entered the Kingdom simply cannot be so understood. Matt. 21:31 means only that the tax collectors and harlots "have a head start along the way that leads to life" (cf. Matt. 7:14). Anyone who presumes to find the presence of the Kingdom in Matt. 23:13 cannot be helped and must be left to his unfortunate opinion.[108] Gösta Lundström, who, like Werner Georg Kümmel, thinks that Jesus understood the Kingdom to be present in his own person, insists: "All the sayings about entering into the Kingdom refer to the coming Kingdom which is often characterized as Life."[109] If the Kingdom were present only in Jesus and his works, one could not yet, of course, enter it.

If Weiss considered these several theories incorrect, he

106. Thus T. W. Manson and G. E. Ladd, for example.
107. See below, pp. 96 f. Cf. *Predigt²*, pp. 111, 112: "The way to Life or the Kingdom leads through the Judgment, where the fate of individuals is decided."
108. *Predigt²*, pp. 79 f.
109. Gösta Lundström, *The Kingdom of God in the Teaching of Jesus*, trans. J. Bulman (Richmond: John Knox, 1963), p. 236. Similarly, Joachim Jeremias, *The Parables of Jesus*, rev. ed. (New York: Scribner's, 1963), p. 125, following Hans Windisch, „Die Sprüche vom Eingehen in das Reiche Gottes," *ZNW* 27 (1928): 163–92. Lundström's book, which bears the same title as Perrin's and was published in English the same year, provides, like Perrin's, a valuable review of the history of the interpretation of Jesus' conception of the Kingdom of God from Weiss to the present. A briefer but excellent survey is also presented by Ridderbos, *Coming of the Kingdom*, pp. xii–xxxi.

did have some alternative suggestions to offer with respect to the main problem. In both editions of the *Predigt* he proposed that Jesus ordinarily thought that the coming of the Kingdom would take place in the future. On a few occasions, however, as noted above,[110] Jesus spoke of the presence of the Kingdom as if it were already an accomplished fact. These utterances appear when Jesus was excited by the victories he and his disciples had won against Satan's household; they reflect moments of sheer enthusiasm in which his mood was temporarily one of exaltation and triumph.[111] They are, however, exceptions to the usual dominical mood expressed in his prayer, "May the Kingdom of God come, deliver us from the Evil One!"[112] It should be noted that the idea of Jesus' different sayings corresponding to different moods is also implicit in Hans Windisch's identification of "wisdom" teachings which, in his judgment, are free from eschatological overtones.[113] Like Weiss, Windisch maintained that Jesus normally thought and spoke of the Kingdom as future.

Weiss's most important theory as to how Jesus could

110. See above, pp. 12 f. It is worth noting here that R. H. Fuller also speaks of the "proleptic" presence not of the Kingdom but of its "powers" or "signs." *The Mission and Achievement of Jesus,* SBT no. 12 (London: SCM, 1954): 29, 50. Here, Fuller, like Bultmann, maintains that Jesus regarded the Kingdom as future, though "dawning." Such, in effect, is Weiss's position, too.

111. Thus in *Predigt²,* p. 70: "Whether he favors the one expression or the other depends on what suits his mood at the time. When storm clouds gather and the lightning flashes on the horizon, one may say: 'A thunder storm is coming.' But one can also say, proleptically: 'It is storming.' Or, again, when the sun shines warm and brightly for the first time, and the first buds begin to swell, one will usually say: 'Spring is near.' But who will restrain his feeling of yearning when it joyfully welcomes in these first signs the whole springtime, as if it were already there with all its splendour?"

112. *Predigt²,* pp. 71, 95 f.

113. Hans Windisch, *The Meaning of the Sermon on the Mount,* trans. S. MacL. Gilmour (Philadelphia: Westminster, 1950), pp. 39 f., 108 f.

have thought the Kingdom both present and future invokes the two-story universe. The Kingdom is present in heaven, but it has not yet come or is just beginning to come on earth.[114] This conception, clearly assumed in Rev. 12:7-12, is also implied in the Matthean version of the Lord's Prayer (Matt. 6:10): in heaven God's will is already done, even though Satan still rules on earth (Luke 4:5-7; Matt. 4:8 f.). Weiss interprets Jesus' healings and exorcisms as a campaign against the kingdom of Satan and on behalf of the Kingdom of God.[115] Perhaps Jesus thought he had overcome Satan at the outset of his ministry.[116] At any rate, "Satan's kingdom is already broken, the rule of God is already gaining ground; but it has not yet become a historical event." God's Kingdom may obtain in heaven, but it has not yet been established on earth.[117] Few of the subsequent interpreters of Jesus' exorcisms or "miracles" hint that there might be any connection between this aspect of his ministry and his other basic concern: preaching in preparation for the coming of the Kingdom. Most of them speak of these activities as manifestations of the "powers of the Kingdom of God."[118] No such expression is to be found in

114. See below, pp. 74 ff.; cf. *Predigt²*, pp. 28 f., 96 ff.
115. See below, pp. 74–81.
116. See below, pp. 80 f.
117. See below, p. 79.
118. E.g., Alan Richardson, *The Miracle Stories of the Gospels* (London: SCM, 1941), p. 38; C. K. Barrett, *Holy Spirit,* p. 68. James M. Robinson urges that the struggle against the demons was an important part of Jesus' historical ministry: *The Problem of History in Mark,* SBT no. 21 (London: SCM, 1957). Like many writers, he assumes—indeed, asserts— that the meaning of Mark 3:27 is that Jesus was "plundering" Satan's household: "Exorcism is specifically designated as 'plundering' in 3:27" (p. 38). Satan had already been bound, so many interpreters assert, at the "temptation" (Mark 1:12 f.). These writers, therefore, do not regard the exorcisms as preparatory to the coming of the Kingdom. Instead, they view them as signs of its presence or "dawning." But exorcism is not *designated* as "plundering" in Mark 3:27. There is another possibility: by casting out demons, Jesus is *binding* Satan's power. (Thus Reginald H.

the synoptic tradition, however. It is an exegetical invention. Weiss takes the position that Jesus regarded his campaign against the demons as preparatory to the coming of the Kingdom, rather than as a sign of its presence or of the presence of its "powers." Once Satan's forces have been overcome on earth, the Kingdom which was already present in heaven could also be established on earth.

Other theories. Since Weiss's time, numerous other explanations have been advanced in regard to the problem: How did Jesus understand the Kingdom to be both present and future? Since Weiss himself did not refer to these more recent types of explanations, one cannot be certain what his reaction to them might have been. If one assumes, as the editors do, that Weiss's historical and exegetical position is to be taken seriously, the following summary and critique of such recent and current theories might be of some value.

Fuller, *Interpreting the Miracles* [Philadelphia: Westminster, 1963], pp. 40 f. Such an interpretation is also suggested by Howard C. Kee, "The Terminology of Mark's Exorcism Stories," *NTS* 14 (1968): 232–46. Kee proposes (with respect to Mark 9:21 ff.) that ἐπιτιμᾶν (= גער) represents "the word of command by which God's agent defeats his enemies, thus preparing for the coming of God's kingdom" [p. 244].) In that case, there would be no need to posit any previous "binding" of Satan by Jesus in the wilderness or elsewhere: the binding is taking place in his exorcisms. The victories over the demons spell Satan's ultimate doom: thus Jesus' prophetic vision of Satan's impending collapse is inspired by the disciples' report of their successes against the demons (Luke 10:17 f.). Ernest Best, *The Temptation and Passion* (New York: Cambridge Univ. Press, 1965) presents the typical speculation that Jesus had defeated Satan in the wilderness, but does not combine this, as do Richardson and Robinson, with realized eschatology. Mauser's brief discussion of the temptation notes that Mark did not understand that Jesus won a victory over Satan in the wilderness or ceased to be tempted by him afterwards; yet Mauser maintains that Mark 3:27 means that Jesus has already "bound" Satan! [Ulrich Mauser, *Christ in the Wilderness,* SBT no. 39 (London: SCM, 1963): 96–102, 130 f.] The assumption that Jesus "defeated" or "bound" Satan in the wilderness or elsewhere at the outset of his ministry does not account for Satan's subsequent vitality, a vitality which Robinson and Mauser recognize, but do not explain.

E. F. Scott, C. H. Dodd, Amos N. Wilder and others have proposed that Jesus' references to the future coming of the Kingdom were "only symbolic" or "stylistic." His apocalyptic imagery was no more than a vehicle for his real meaning, which was that the Kingdom of God had already come. Bultmann explains Jesus' eschatological language as mythological garments in which he cloaked his true (existentialist) understanding of the human situation. These writers, however, appear more interested in explaining Jesus' futuristic expectation away, than in showing how he could have believed the Kingdom both present and future.[119] Moreover, any "symbolic" theory leaves unex-

---

119. Bultmann is less guilty of this procedure than the others: but even he sometimes presents Jesus as teacher of the timeless (or perpetually recurrent) existentialist *now* of decision. In the process, the future coming of the Kingdom of God disappears. Thus, e.g., *Jesus and the Word*, trans. L. P. Smith and E. H. Lantero (New York: Scribner's, 1934, 1958), pp. 51 f., 131. As Ernst Lohmeyer pointed out in *Kerygma and Myth* 1:128, Bultmann's demythologizing sometimes means, in practice, "the abolition of the myth," despite his announced intention to interpret the meaning of the myth. But one should give Bultmann credit for attempting, in general, as he says in response to Lohmeyer (ibid., p. 205), to *expose* the meaning of New Testament eschatology, in contrast to most of the interpreters before (and after) Weiss and Schweitzer who have been more concerned to *dispose* of it. Weiss took note of the mixture of subjective and dogmatic with exegetical considerations evident in the interest many interpreters showed in promoting the idea that Jesus thought the Kingdom to be present: *Predigt²*, pp. 71, 73–85. See also Martin Werner, *Die Entstehung des christlichen Dogmas*, 2nd ed. (Bern: Haupt, 1953), pp. 36–52; G. R. Beasley-Murray, *Jesus and the Future* (London: Macmillan, 1954), pp. 1–32, 183 ff; W. G. Kümmel, *Promise and Fulfillment*, pp. 143 ff., and "Futuristic and Realized Eschatology in the Earliest Stages of Chirstianity," *JR* 43 (1963): 303–308; Erich Grässer, *Das Problem der Parusieverzögerung in den Synoptischen Evangelien und in der Apostelgeschichte*, 2nd ed. (Berlin: Töpelmann, 1960), pp. 12–15. Among various journal articles: Clarence T. Craig, "Realized Eschatology," *JBL* 56 (1937): 17–26; Paul Schubert, "The Synoptic Gospels and Eschatology," *JBR* 14 (1946): 155–57; Millar Burrows, "Thy Kingdom Come," *JBL* 74 (1955): 1–8; and R. H. Hiers, "Eschatology and Methodology," *JBL* 85 (1966): 175–184.

plained why Jesus should have wished to obscure his "real" message that the Kingdom had already arrived by speaking of its coming in the future. Even Harnack, as early as 1900, rejected a similar theory: "This was no mere image or empty idea; it was a truth which he saw and felt most vividly."[120]

Harnack's solution to the problem was different: Jesus believed that the Kingdom was already present as the rule of God in the hearts of individuals. He also looked for its dramatic establishment in the future. *We* can see that these ideas are incompatible, Harnack urged, but Jesus simply failed to perceive the contradiction![121] It is evident that neither Jesus nor the evangelists felt it necessary to explain such a contradiction. But it may be that there was no contradiction to explain! The claim that Jesus viewed the Kingdom of God as his rule in the hearts of men does not carry the weight of probability.[122]

Some other interpreters divide Jesus' ministry into two periods. In the first part of his ministry, T. W. Manson proposed, Jesus spoke of the Kingdom as a coming future event. In the second period (after Peter's "confession"), he spoke of it as having already come.[123] Herman Ridderbos, on the other hand, finds that Jesus spoke of it as present in the first part of his ministry, but in the latter part came to think of it as something which was still to be fulfilled.[124] However, the synoptic evidence cannot be sorted out into any two such periods without arbitrarily rearrang-

120. Harnack, *What is Christianity?*, p. 53.
121. Ibid., pp. 54 f.
122. See R. H. Hiers, "Why Will They Not Say, 'Lo, here!' or 'There!'?", *JAAR* 35 (1967): 379–384.
123. T. W. Manson, *The Teaching of Jesus* (New York: Cambridge Univ. Press, 1951), pp. 119–31.
124. Ridderbos, *Coming of the Kingdom*, p. 468; and, earlier, H. J. Holtzmann.

ing the text in accordance with the result one has determined to establish.

The proposal has been made, most recently by George Eldon Ladd, that the term ἡ βασιλεία (like its Semitic counterparts) has two distinguishable meanings: The reign, kingly power, rule, sovereignty, dominion or *Herrschaft* of God, which, presumably, for Jesus and his contemporaries was always present; and the realm, kingdom, domain or *Reich* of God, which Jesus expected in the future. The sayings about the present Kingdom refer to the eternal reign of God; the future sayings to the realm, which has yet to be established on earth.[125] But in that case, one must ask, in what sense can it be said that God "reigns" on earth? *If* God reigns on earth, his Kingdom is already established here: the realm of earth is his. But precisely the point at issue is whether or not God reigns on earth. Weiss's study suggests that Jesus believed that Satan still ruled here, even if his power was being overcome. Moreover, Ladd himself holds this view only inconsistently, for later in his book he speaks of the present realm of God as "the new Age" which Jesus declared men could enter.

Joachim Jeremias recognizes a distinction between the "Kingdom of God" and the "Messianic" or "New Age." The Kingdom of God will be ushered in by the Judgment at some time in the future. But, Jeremias maintains, Jesus understood and proclaimed that the "Messianic Age" or "New Age" had come.[126] It is remarkable that Jeremias seems to feel no need to justify this distinction, to explain the relation (if any) between these various terms, or to account for the expression "Messianic Age," which does not

125. Ladd, *Jesus and Kingdom,* esp. pp. 118–145; also his article, "The Kingdom of God: Reign or Realm?", *JBL* 81 (1962): 230–238. This interpretation was pioneered by Gustaf Dalman: see Perrin, *Kingdom of God,* pp. 23–28.
126. Jeremias, *Parables* (1963), pp. 118, 122, 151 f., 226 f.

appear in the synoptic tradition. No distinction between the "Coming Age" and any preliminary "Messianic Age" was known in Jewish thought before the end of the first century A.D.[127] Nowhere in the New Testament is it stated by Jesus or anyone else that the "New Age" has come. Furthermore, Jeremias does not succeed in maintaining a distinction between these categories. In at least one place he declares that the "Messianic Age" is still to come, and elsewhere intimates that Jesus thought that the Kingdom of God was beginning to be present,[128] even though the Judgment had not yet taken place.

Finally,[129] Hans Conzelmann has suggested a distinction

127. Thus Volz, *Eschatologie,* pp. 71–77.
128. Jeremias, *Parables* (1963), pp. 149, 152 f. Here Jeremias seems to use the terms "Messianic Age" and "Kingdom of God" synonomously.
129. There were still other theories, but like the "symbolic" theory, most of them seem to have been aimed at disposing of the futuristic expectation, rather than explaining the relation between the conceptions, imputed to Jesus, of a present and a future coming of the Kingdom. There were, for instance, the theories (both advocated by C. H. Dodd, among others) that many of the futuristic sayings were interpolated by the church, or that some of them referred, originally, to future historical or political crises which Jesus saw looming on the horizon, such as the destruction of Jerusalem by the Romans. Oscar Cullmann seeks to resolve the tension between present and future by claiming that "in Christ time is divided anew." (*Christ and Time,* trans. F. V. Filson [Philadelphia: Westminster, 1950], p. 84). Various other writers attempt to show that for Jesus and his disciples, present and future had no temporal meaning. Thus, for example, Perrin, *Rediscovering,* pp. 204 ff., insists (as the nineteenth century liberal writers had before him) that the Kingdom of God meant primarily human religious "experience": ibid., pp. 67, 74, 82, 89, 126, 151 f. Recently Pannenberg has attempted to explain the juxtaposition of present and future: Wolfhart Pannenberg, "Appearance as the Arrival of the Future," *JAAR* 35 (1967): 111–113. The "presence" or "appearance" of the Kingdom (or "Reign") of God, he declares, takes shape whenever men respond in obedience to God. Like Harnack, Pannenberg tends to equate "God" and "Kingdom of God"; also, the latter's proposal that God's Reign is present in men's obedience is reminiscent of the former's definition of the Kingdom as the rule of God in the hearts of men. Harnack, however, regarded the futurity of the Kingdom as unessential and thus expendable, whereas Pannenberg defends its

between the "manifestation" of the Kingdom of God in Jesus' ministry and its future coming. He attributes this distinction to Luke, and perhaps also to Jesus. It was the manifestation of the Kingdom that was present, not the Kingdom itself. The former was the "main declaration" (of Jesus?); the latter was less important.[130] Earlier, Martin Dibelius had interpreted Luke 17:20 f. similarly: Jesus proclaimed the future coming of the Kingdom; but he, himself, his message and deeds, were the "signs of the Kingdom" already present "in your midst."[131]

It is remarkable that so many different theories have been advanced, and that none of them has gained general support. In each instance (except for C. H. Dodd) it is conceded that Jesus expected the Kingdom to come in the future. What is problematic is the question how he may also have understood it to be present. Perhaps it would be timely to ask, once more, whether he thought of it as pres-

fundamental importance in Jesus' message and ministry. See also W. Pannenberg et al., *Revelation as History,* trans. David Granskou (New York: Macmillan, 1968), pp. 142–45, and Pannenberg's more recent collection of essays, *Theology and the Kingdom of God* (Philadelphia: Westminster, 1969), esp. pp. 52–57.

130. Hans Conzelmann, *The Theology of St. Luke,* trans. G. Buswell (New York: Harper, 1960), pp. 122 f. See also p. 105. Similarly in his article "Jesus Christus" [RGG³, 3 (1959): 641–45], Conzelmann urged that the eschatological salvation proclaimed and expected by Jesus was present to his hearers and is accessible for "us" today. Salvation is known existentially in the present moment: the "new time" is here, though the kingdom of God has not yet come (p. 644). Cf. Jeremias' questionable distinction between the "New Age" and the Kingdom of God. Conzelmann's dismissal of the imminent expectation from Lukan eschatology has been challenged recently in two excellent articles: Fred O. Francis, "Eschatology and History in Luke-Acts," *JAAR* 37 (1969): 49–63; Charles H. Talbert, "The Redaction Critical Quest for Luke the Theologian," *Jesus and Man's Hope,* ed. D. G. Buttrick (Pittsburgh: Pittsburgh Theological Seminary, 1970), pp. 171–222.

131. Martin Dibelius, *Jesus,* trans. C. B. Hedrick and F. C. Grant (Philadelphia: Westminster, 1949), pp. 73 ff.

ent in any way, other than in heaven, whence it would soon come to earth. There can be little doubt that Jesus regarded certain preliminary and preparatory eschatological phenomena as present or being realized. Elijah had appeared;[132] the final campaign against Satan's household was under way; the preaching of repentance in prospect of the nearness of the Judgment and the Kingdom had begun. But did Jesus also believe that the Kingdom of God had come?

Because this network of problems—involving the Kingdom of God, the self-interpretation of Jesus, the relation of Jesus' message to that of the early church, the issue of whether Jesus was "wrong" in his fundamental expectation, and so on—has dominated twentieth century study of Jesus, it is useful to read for oneself the little book that set the whole discussion in motion.

THE FIRST AND REVISED EDITIONS

The question will naturally arise why the revised and expanded edition of 1900 was not translated instead of the first edition.[133] It is the judgment of the editors that the first edition presents Weiss's thesis more clearly and forcefully than the second. It obviously does so more compactly: 67 as compared with 210 pages. The additional excurses[134] and background material with respect to Old Testament and Jewish concepts of the Kingdom[135] presented in the

132. See J. A. T. Robinson, "Elijah, John and Jesus" (1958) in his *Twelve New Testament Studies,* SBT no. 34 (London: SCM, 1962): 28–52.

133. See also above, pp. 18–21.

134. These treat, respectively, the Beatitudes; Matt. 6:33 and the δικαιοσύνη θεοῦ; Matt. 11:12, Luke 16:16; Mark 10:45 and the sayings at the Last Supper; and the nonmessianic Son of man sayings.

135. The second edition constitutes primarily an explication, an amplification, an intensification, and an adjustment of the argument of the first edition. An illustration of the sort of expansion Weiss provides can be taken from *Predigt²,* pp. 30 ff. There Weiss traces the dualism of apoca-

second edition are still of value, but Weiss's argument neither derives from nor rests upon this sort of support, and its absence from the first edition here translated is an advantage rather than a detriment to his reader today.

In a very few instances, Weiss modified his interpretation to some degree in *Predigt²*. An illustration lies in his treatment of the parables. In *Predigt¹*, Weiss treats the parables of the sower, the mustard seed, the leaven and the tares as if they had nothing to do with the Kingdom of God, but only, as he says, with the fate of the proclaimed word.[136] Any reference to the Kingdom is by evangelistic accretion from Mark 4:11. However, in *Predigt²*, the parables of the mustard seed and the leaven are treated differently.[137] Here they are admitted to have a connection with the Kingdom of God and only illicit notions of growth or development are denied. Their meaning for the Kingdom lies in their contrasting smallness and largeness, insignificance and overwhelming significance. And, in the second edition, the parable of the seed growing secretly is finally dealt with.[138] In it, the presence of the Kingdom is again acknowledged and the idea of development rejected. Other such instances of modification are indicated in the editors' footnotes.

lyptic eschatology back not to the Old Testament, but to Persian "Parseeism" (sc. Zoroastrianism: Weiss's confusion of Zoroastrianism *per se* with the Parsees was a common error of his time. "Parsee," of course, is a name properly applied only to those Persians who fled to India in the seventh and eighth centuries to avoid Muslim persecution. The Parsees did maintain their Zoroastrian faith, however.). Frequently Weiss's expansions of this sort rest upon scholarly judgments and an antiquated bibliography which can no longer stand critical scrutiny. Hence, since Weiss's argument is independent of this kind of material and is so presented in *Predigt¹*, the editors adjudged the lack of these expansions a virtue rather than a vice in the present translation.

136. See below, pp. 72 f.
137. *Predigt²*, pp. 82 f.
138. *Predigt²*, pp. 84 f.

Perhaps it would be well to add at this point once again that it was Weiss's need to make a strong negative case against the Ritschlian school of thought in the first edition which made him reticent to admit the presence of any allusion to the Kingdom of God in those parables. Precisely those pericopes were, after all, the main sources of support used by the liberal theologians to buttress their position, and, given the strength of that view, Weiss could scarcely get an adequate hearing for his alternate position if he allowed even the possibility that the position they espoused had exegetical plausibility. In the second edition of his work, it was possible for him to relax his treatment of the texts somewhat. His point had been made; the frontal assault was over. But fundamentally, Weiss had seen little reason to alter the main outlines of his original discussion.

Another reason for translating the first edition is that the second has recently been reprinted,[139] and so will be available to those readers who wish to examine Weiss's more detailed treatment of the subject.

Weiss does take occasion in the second edition to elaborate a point which is only briefly suggested in our present work, namely, that many of Jesus' sayings were *not* determined or conditioned by his eschatological beliefs.[140] Jesus experienced the prophetic spirit only intermittently. In its absence Jesus felt the love, goodness and mercy of God shining through the clouds like the sun. At such moments

> The lilies of the field speak to him, through their beauty, of the never-tiring providence of the Creator. In the eye of a child, he catches a glimpse of the nature of God, who loves children, and above his head he watches the movement of the stars as they had been moving since eternity.[141]

139. See note 8 above, p. 6.
140. See above, p. 20.
141. *Predigt*[2], p. 135.

At such moments he no longer was thinking of the end of the world. "Then he is no longer the dark and harsh prophet, but a man among men, a child of God among children of God." "Out of such a mood were born those sayings and parables whose freshness will never grow old, in which there is little trace of world-weariness and asceticism, of the end of the world and of judgment."[142] Curiously, however, Weiss does not specify which among Jesus' sayings and parables fall into this category.

One might wish to suggest, Weiss continues, that in such sayings one encounters the true inward nature of Jesus. "But the historian will also readily recognize that this is only *one* side of the picture that tradition offers us. . . . His figure encounters us on the pages of the Gospels in storm and strife; in the storm of prophetic inspiration, and in struggle with opponents. . . ."[143] A great many of his ethical ideas are expressed in the discussions with these opponents, especially the Pharisees. For the most part, Jesus' antipharisaic ethic is not related to his eschatological preaching, as, for example, in the case of the dispute about hand-washing. "When Jesus defends the divine institution of marriage or the sanctity of oaths against the frivolous casuistry of the rabbis, he undoubtedly speaks, to be sure, as a prophet, but more as a preacher and reformer than as a herald of the Kingdom of God."[144]

The "double-love commandment," which is usually regarded as the basic core (*Kern und Stern*) of his proclamation, is also independent of the eschatological viewpoint. Actually, it was formulated by a scribe, not by Jesus; and it does not appear in the Sermon on the Mount or, really, in the actual "proclamation" of Jesus at all. Nevertheless,

142. Ibid.
143. *Predigt²,* p. 136.
144. *Predigt²,* p. 137.

because it can be detached from his messianic preaching, it is serviceable as a regulative principle for Christian ethics in all times to come.[145] Jesus' "new ethic," however, was preached as the condition for entrance into the Kingdom, not as the ethic of the realized Kingdom of God. "His (Jesus') demands are not derived from some idea of a perfect human society or from generally valid ethical norms. They are, rather, grounded in the fearful gravity of the present moment. The greatest crisis in world history stands before the door."[146] This is the penitential ethic of preparation described above.[147]

In effect, then, Weiss makes clear in *Predigt²* what was earlier hinted in *Predigt¹:* that Jesus' teaching and outlook, especially concerning God's love for his creatures and the commandment of love as basis for the relationships among men, were not entirely grounded upon the eschatological expectation. Nevertheless, it is as clear in the second as in the first edition that Weiss found Jesus' proclamation set forth in the context of that expectation. Apart from a few moments of prophetic inspiration when Jesus spoke of it *as if* it had already come, he consistently looked for the coming of the Kingdom in the near future.

NOTE BY THE TRANSLATORS-EDITORS

As an aid to readers who might wish to pursue these references, the secondary literature and authors mentioned by Weiss have been included. It is not necessary, however,

---

145. *Predigt²*, pp. 137 f.

146. *Predigt²*, p. 138.

147. See above, pp. 10 f. Few interpreters have been willing to concede that Jesus' ethic was either a "penitential" or an "interim" ethic, but none has succeeded in demonstrating the inaccuracy of the characterization either. Cf. R. H. Hiers, "Interim Ethics," *Theology and Life* 9 (1966): 220–233.

to read Weiss with this material at hand. His position in this volume speaks for itself.

Since the discussion of many points has moved on since 1892, the editors have provided a number of additional footnotes to indicate significant references, including several places where Weiss himself corrected or further developed certain points in his own later writings, especially in *Predigt²*. Obviously much has to be omitted, since a substantial portion of later New Testament research is adumbrated in *Predigt¹*. All of the additions to the text and notes by the translators-editors are in brackets. The chapter headings, except for the eleventh which Weiss himself had included, have been added by the editors, who have also introduced a number of new paragraph divisions within the text. Some attempt has been made to standardize the translation of important words: for instance, *Herrschaft* is generally rendered as "rule" and *Reich* as "kingdom"; *Stimmung* as "attitude"; and *verwirklichen* as "to actualize."

Obviously, Weiss was in no position to answer definitively all questions about Jesus' eschatological beliefs. But he presented many of these questions clearly for the first time, without regard to the dogmatic fears and desires of conservative or liberal theologies. Those who wish to carry the discussion of these questions forward to a still more precise account of the matter can hardly do better than to begin with Weiss's presentation.

JESUS' PROCLAMATION
OF
THE KINGDOM OF GOD

by Johannes Weiss

PREFACE

The immediate occasion for publishing this essay, which I drafted some time ago, was presented to me by the appearance of the books by Schmoller and Issel concerning the doctrine of the Kingdom of God in the New Testament, both of which appeared in Leiden in 1891 as prize-winning essays. I welcome, particularly in Schmoller's book, the same interest which I am pursuing, namely, to make clear the completely apocalyptic and eschatological character of Jesus' idea of the Kingdom. Since both of these books will probably evoke a lively debate, I should not wish to keep back my views on this question which I have developed independently, and I hope that I have adduced a number of supplementary points which will help to clarify this important question.

JOHANNES WEISS

Göttingen,
January 24, 1892

[INTRODUCTION]

One of the most gratifying and promising aspects of recent theology[1] is its serious attention to and emphasis upon the concept "Kingdom of God." Even to common historical sense it must appear appropriate when describing the positive character of the Christian religion and the historical circumstances under which it arose to take as the point of departure and center of systematic theology the main ideas of Jesus' proclamation, rather than Paul's doctrine of justification. This likewise gives a more satisfactory basis for a really systematic arrangement of the series of Christian concepts which theology has to offer with respect to the special tasks for our time. It is possible on this basis to include in a unified perspective both "dogmatics" and "ethics," which otherwise always more or less fall apart, at least where systematic theology is constructed on the pattern of the doctrine of justification. The artificial isolation of religious experiences, "of the action of God upon men," from the religious-ethical reactions of individuals is a necessary consequence of the separation of the two disciplines which in turn follows from the mechanical demarcation between justification and new life. The application of this important orientation will even prove useful for practical theology and the preaching of the Gospel. For it is an open secret that preaching and instruction which proceed according to

1. [By "recent," "modern," or "the newer" theology, Weiss refers to that theological movement in late nineteenth century German theology of which Albrecht Ritschl is probably the most influential representative. See above, pp. 4 ff., 16 ff. Ritschl's conceptions of justification, ethics, and the Kingdom of God are reviewed briefly by H. Richard Niebuhr, *Christ and Culture* (New York: Harper, 1951), pp. 96–101.]

the pattern of the *ordo salutis* in the old Protestant sense, bounce off the majority of our contemporaries without effect. Such is the case for several reasons. First of all, the organic connection between the religious good and the ethical ideal does not stand out clearly enough. Moreover, the doctrine of redemption which is defined over against a general conception of sin is not concrete, and therefore not practical enough. Finally, the factor of gradual education through God's grace must necessarily be neglected where all one's energy is directed toward presenting the fundamental act of justification and forgiveness of sins.

More recent dogmatics (exhibiting an enormous step forward) shows that it no longer pictures justification as a detached experience, as the acceptance of a sinner who until then had been completely estranged from God, but shows instead how the *Christian* born, raised, and developed within the congregation may, despite his sin, hope for the grace of God. But even so, there are still difficulties and dangers in the use of the word "justification." This word always necessarily calls forth the image of a single, dramatic act of pardon ($\delta\iota\kappa\alpha\acute{\iota}\omega\sigma\iota\varsigma$). But then if something of the sort is not experienced, what emerges will be either pietistic self-torment, or indifference toward an unintelligible doctrine. Preaching surely will not miss its mark, however, if it calls men seriously and enthusiastically into the Kingdom of God, into the company of those who entrust themselves to God as King and Leader of their lives, and commit their energies to his service. It will not miss its mark if it can show how limited yet how abundant, how simple and yet how immeasurably difficult, how grave and yet how exalted are the tasks which God gives to his servants in this Kingdom. And it must show that these tasks are possible only to one who feeds his soul with power from on high, by means of which he, himself a king, yet humble and joyous as a child, allows God to lead and form his life. We are not today in the kind of situation where our preaching has only to direct a surplus of religion into the correct paths. Our principal task does not consist in finding some way to solve the religious questions that people find perplexing. Rather, the real problem is, first of all, to reawaken religion. But we can never do this if we immediately confront our congregations with the greatest and most difficult things in Christianity, which require sensitive and believing minds if they are to be understood, and proceed deductively to derive from these the requirements for the moral life. Instead, we can succeed only if we introduce them inductively to Christian living (both ethical *and* religious) in its simplest and most concrete form. Then it will come about, when we once more have a Christian community in which new and tender life is sheltered and can prosper, that "faith" in the higher sense, as the heroes of our religion know it, will grow up of its own accord in minds prepared for it.

From what has been said, it is sufficiently evident that we ought to be grateful for the new emphasis upon this central idea of Jesus. It therefore seems all the more necessary, however, to submit the historical foundations of this concept to a thorough investigation. Every dogmatics which employs Biblical concepts is always in the more or less clearly perceived danger of stripping these concepts of their original historical character by reinterpreting or converting them to new purposes in accordance with new viewpoints. There can be no objection to this procedure as such. For in all areas of the intellectual life, it is necessarily the case that words and concepts are transformed by later generations into new coinage and new meaning. Theology must insist only on one thing if it wants to remain clear concerning itself and conscious of its procedures, namely, that one should acknowledge whether and how far we today are removed from the original meaning of the concepts, and that one should declare, for the sake of clarity, that he wishes to issue the old coinage at a new rate of exchange. In this regard, it might not be superfluous if we attempt once more to identify the original historical meaning which Jesus connected with the words "Kingdom of God," and if we do it with special care lest we import modern, or at any rate alien, ideas into Jesus' thought-world.

1. [EVALUATION OF THE SOURCES]

The problem is already complicated enough because of the nature of the sources.[2] The contemporary state of Gospel criticism justifies our excluding the Gospel of John almost totally from our investigation. It is dispensable to a large degree from our study since it furnishes few direct sayings concerning the Kingdom of God. But even the synoptic Gospels can be used only with certain qualifications, for at precisely those points which relate to our theme we have to take note of secondary displacement of the original material. Many today would also concur in regarding Mark, or at least a writing "A" of like scope and composition to Mark, as the skeleton for both of the other Gospels.[3] In addition, one may venture to acknowledge a source "Q" which contained predominantly sayings and which can be—though it has admittedly not yet been—reconstructed from Matthew and Luke. And one may also posit a special source for Luke "LQ" containing narratives, parables, and sayings. Furthermore, over against a recent tendency in criticism, I believe it must be maintained that

2. [Cf. *Predigt²*, pp. 36–40.]
3. [Weiss, like the later European form critics, considered Mark's chronology unreliable: *Predigt²*, pp. 38 f.]

Luke is not dependent on Matthew (and vice versa). On this point I regard as conclusive, among other things, the evidence set forth by Pfleiderer[4] which indicates that our first Gospel [Matthew] was composed at a very late date: it already contains signs of the church's becoming catholic, and it points in the direction of the Apologists.[5]

But even so, there are certain passages of this Gospel—to be selected with prudence of course—which are customarily preferred in construing Jesus' conception of the Kingdom of God;[6] particularly the explanation of the parable of the tares and the Matthean redaction of the parable itself (Matt. 13:24–30, 36–43), the simile of the fishnet (Matt. 13:47–50), and also the redaction of the Judgment Scene (Matt. 25:31–46), which belong, in the judgment of many scholars, to the latest components of the Gospel. These, consequently, cannot serve as direct sources for us because they contain a conception of the Kingdom of God formed from the standpoint of the later community by analogy to certain Pauline formulations. Matthew 13:41 distinguishes a $\beta\alpha\sigma\iota\lambda\epsilon i\alpha$ of the Son of man (cf. John 18:36 f.)—the *ecclesia visibilis*—from the $\beta\alpha\sigma\iota\lambda\epsilon i\alpha$ $\tau o\hat{v}$ $\pi\alpha\tau\rho\acute{o}s$. Until then, the righteous were to dwell together with the sinners in the Kingdom of Christ, under the lordship of the Son of man; but with the $\sigma\nu\nu\tau\acute{e}\lambda\epsilon\iota\alpha$ $\tau o\hat{v}$ $\alpha i\hat{\omega}\nu os$

4. Otto Pfleiderer, *Das Urchristentum, seine Schriften und Lehren, in geschichtlichem Zusammenhang beschrieben* (Berlin: G. Reimer, 1887), pp. 538 ff. [Trans. W. Montgomery, *Primitive Christianity: Its Writings and Teachings in Their Historical Connections,* 2 vols. (New York: G. P. Putnam's Sons, and London: Williams & Norgate, 1906, 1909), 2: 382 ff.]

5. Although I certainly consider it important, I shall pass by for the time being the question of the sources of Mark or "A" as hardly yet soluble. For an assessment of this question, see especially Bernhard Weiss, *Das Marcusevangelium und seine synoptische Parallelen erklärt* (Berlin: W. Hertz, 1872).

6. [Cf. *Predigt²,* pp. 40–49.]

(Matt. 13:39), when Christ as βασιλεύς will sit in judgment (Matt. 25:31), the righteous will enter into life (Matt. 25:46) or inherit the Kingdom which the Father had prepared for them from the foundation of the world. This conception of a βασιλεία τοῦ Χριστοῦ which then will be separate from the βασιλεία θεοῦ is reported to us first by Paul (Col. 1:13 f.; 1 Cor. 15:24 f.), who, however, expresses here only one common early Christian view. In any case, it was invented from the standpoint of the ancient congregations who, in the exalted κύριος, recognize Christ, the divine regent of the world, commissioned to reign for a time as God's representative. Furthermore, they hope for his definitive overthrow of God's enemies until, after a complete victory, the strong hand of God himself will take up the reins once more. Because these conceptions belong within this thought-world of early Christianity, and proceed from belief in the Exalted One (Acts 2:36), we cannot consider them among the authentic statements of Jesus.

Equally little do I regard the characteristics which might perhaps be derived from the phrase βασιλεία τῶν οὐρανῶν as features of the original idea. An expression which appears only in Matthew and John (3:5),[7] but not in the Logia "Q", e.g., Matt. 12:28, presents little claim to be regarded as original, and one is continually constrained to declare it one of Matthew's most characteristic ideas. It appears, indeed, to be connected to that general shift in the conception of the Kingdom of God which has just been

7. [The expression "Kingdom of Heaven" in John 3:5 is attested by only a few manuscript traditions. Its common usage in Matthew is now generally regarded as a circumlocution or substitute for the divine name, one of several Jewish features of the "First" evangelist. Weiss denies the validity of G. Dalman's proposal that Jesus himself used the expression as a circumlocution, noting that the term "Kingdom of God" appears regularly in the earliest sources, Mark and "Q" (e.g., Matt. 21:31 and 6:10). See *Predigt²*, p. 43.]

described. For however one may interpret the genitive form of τῶν οὐρανῶν, whether as a designation of place, or as genitive of origin, or as simple subjective genitive (essentially equivalent to τοῦ θεοῦ in Luke 15:18, 21), the βασιλεία still always appears to be thought of as completely transcendent and distinct from the present βασιλεία of Christ on earth. In no case, therefore, may one regard this peculiarity of the first evangelist as the viewpoint of Jesus himself.

Likewise, another preliminary remark concerning the parables is in order, especially concerning the form in which they appear in Matthew. A great many of them are introduced by a formula such as ἡ βασιλεία τ. θεοῦ (τ. οὐρ.) ὁμοία ἐστιν, etc. It is generally recognized that this comparison is to be understood only in a very loose sense. The translation "With the Kingdom of God, it is as with . . ." might well approximate the vagueness of the formula.[8] More important is the fact that *the whole point of view* which regards the parables as a description of conditions within the Kingdom of God cannot be taken as binding for our strictly historical way of thinking. That method is derived from a saying of Jesus in Mark 4:11, the present textual form of which departs from the original of "A" which can still be recognized today from the Matthean and Lukan parallels.[9] According to the testimony of both these references (Matt. 13:10-13; Luke 8:9-10), the verse originally read: ὑμῖν δέδοται γνῶναι τὰ μυστήρια τῆς βασιλείας τοῦ θεοῦ, ἐκείνοις δὲ ἐν παραβολαῖς. One gains the impression—and this is certainly the meaning of the evangelists—that the parables which are not compre-

8. [Weiss elaborates this point in *Predigt*², pp. 45 ff. Joachim Jeremias offers the same proposal: *The Parables of Jesus*, rev. ed. (New York: Scribner's, 1963), p. 225.]
9. Cf. my essay on the parable discourse in Mark in *Studien und Kritiken*, 1891 ["*Die Parabelrede bei Marcus*," pp. 289-321], pp. 297-305.

hended by the people are supposed to present "secrets of the Kingdom of God." But how this expression is to be understood is not entirely clear. Usually one thinks of the "secret laws which are valid in the Kingdom of God" or the "secret means by which the rule of God will be established." In any case, what is intended is a description of the circumstances of the Kingdom of God, which is regarded, in some way or other, as coincident with the concern of the Gospel or with the community of the disciples. This saying in Mark inspired the other evangelists to attach this formula to a wide range of other parables. But now it is to be observed that: 1) a great many parables which are introduced in this manner have nothing at all to do with the Kingdom of God or can be related to it only with difficulty; and 2) in many cases the evangelists themselves abandon that formula and along with it the basic viewpoint as to the meaning of the parables. Because of this situation and because of the often extremely clumsy style of the introduction, we are obliged to disregard this interpretation entirely and to explain these parables, first of all, without regard to the Kingdom of God and, conversely, the idea of the Kingdom of God without regard to those parables.[10]

Finally, it will be necessary to be careful in our historical description not to let ourselves be influenced by the language and religious outlook of the Fourth Gospel, which—though one is usually unaware of it—governs our religious and scholarly manner of speaking and thinking to a very considerable degree. Compare, for example, the systems of Schleiermacher, Ritschl, Kaftan and others.[11]

10. From this, one may suspect that the expression in Mark 4:11, which, because of the phrase ἐν παραβολαῖς, is applied by the evangelists to the parables, originally had a different meaning. Cf. *Studien und Kritiken*, 1891, pp. 303 ff. (See n. 9 above.) [And cf. *Predigt²*, pp. 82 ff.]

11. [Were he writing today, Weiss might well include Dodd and possibly Bultmann in this list. Cf. *Predigt²*, pp. 60–64.]

2. [REPENTANCE AND THE COMING OF THE KINGDOM][12]

According to the oldest report, Jesus appeared in Galilee with a message, the content of which was briefly set forth in "A" as follows: μετανοεῖτε· ἤγγικεν γὰρ ἡ βασιλεία τοῦ θεοῦ.[13]

This brief summary seems to be established even more firmly by the Sayings source "Q". Thus in Jesus' instructions to his disciples on the occasion of his sending them forth, which seems to be reproduced from the same source, we read:

πορευόμενοι δὲ κηρύσσετε λέγοντες· (ὅτι) ἤγγικεν ἡ βασιλεία τῶν οὐρανῶν (Matt. 10:7).

καὶ λέγετε αὐτοῖς· ἤγγικεν ἐφ᾽ ὑμᾶς ἡ βασιλεία τοῦ θεοῦ (Luke 10:9).

πλὴν τοῦτο γινώσκετε, ὅτι ἤγγικεν ἡ βασιλεία τοῦ θεοῦ (Luke 10:11).

The meaning of this well-attested proclamation of Jesus and his disciples seems quite clear: the Kingdom (or the

12. [On this general section, cf. *Predigt²*, pp. 65–99.]

13. Our present text in Mark is enlarged by the Paulinizing formulation: πεπλήρωται ὁ καιρὸς καὶ ἤγγικεν ἡ βασιλεία τοῦ θεοῦ. μετανοεῖτε καὶ πιστεύετε ἐν τῷ εὐαγγελίῳ τοῦ θεοῦ. [Mark 1:15]. The reading given above is also supported by Matt. 4:17. To be sure, it might be possible that a recollection of the original wording in "A" may be preserved in the codices A and D, and in it⁵, vg, pesh, aeth, and goth (if one does not opt for the reading given in the text; in that case, what has been said would also be true of our present Marcan text): instead of εὐαγγέλιον τοῦ θεοῦ, they read εὐαγγέλιον τῆς βασιλείας τοῦ θεοῦ. If one considers, of course, the fact that Matthew twice has the phrase εὐαγγέλιον τῆς βασιλείας in other passages (Matt. 4:23; 9:35), and that Luke also (4:43; 8:1) speaks of εὐαγγελίζεσθαι τὴν βασιλείαν, one might come to suspect that the reading in "A" was originally only κηρύσσων τὸ εὐαγγέλιον τῆς βασιλείας λέγων· μετανοεῖτε. Then the formula ἤγγικεν, etc., would not have been in "A" at all (it is missing also in Mark 6:12), but would have been supplied by the last editor of Mark in accordance with a saying which appears several times in the Logia.

rule) of God has drawn so near that it stands at the door. Therefore, while the βασιλεία is not yet *here,* it is extremely near.[14] Moreover, there is yet another saying reminiscent of Luke 10:9. In addition to ἤγγικεν ἐφ' ὑμᾶς ἡ βασιλεία τοῦ θεοῦ, there is in Matt. 12:28 (and in the parallel passage, Luke 11:20) the expression: ἔφθασεν ἐφ' ὑμᾶς ἡ βασιλεία τοῦ θεοῦ. The similarity of both ideas is still more surprising if one thinks of the context. Luke 11 says: "If I, by the finger of God, i.e., with real success, cast out demons, then, as you yourselves can infer, ἔφθασεν ἡ βασιλεία τοῦ θεοῦ." Likewise in the speech at the sending out of the disciples, the term ἤγγικεν follows directly upon the successful healings by the disciples.[15] The people among whom the disciples carry out their mission are expected to infer and perceive from the healings that the Kingdom of God is close by (or perhaps even already present?). It is customarily assumed that ἤγγικεν is to be differentiated linguistically and materially from ἔφθασεν.

But is the difference between these two terms really so great? In the case of Dan. 4:8, the same verb מטא is translated by Theodotion with ἔφθασε, but by the LXX with ἤγγισε. From the context it turns out that the verb in question, which the LXX renders in other passages with παρῆν (Dan. 7:13) or with ἥξει (Dan. 4:21), signifies not merely an approach, but a real coming into contact.[16] If we

14. [Cf. Predigt², pp. 69–73. The expression "at the door," as Weiss doubtless realized, comes from the apocalyptic prediction in Mark 13:29 = Matt. 24:33 which refers to that time in the future when the Son of man *will be* near (cf. Luke 21:31—the Kingdom of God), and is, in its present structure, quite probably secondary. Here Weiss simply uses it to symbolize the imminent expectation which he finds evidenced in the message of Jesus and his disciples to their contemporaries.]

15. [See, e.g., Luke 10:9.]

16. The relevant data are as follows: Dan. 4:8: ורומה ימטא לשמיא, LXX: ἡ κορυφὴ αὐτοῦ ἤγγισεν ἕως τ. οὐρανοῦ, Theod.: τὸ ὕψος αὐτοῦ ἔφθασεν ἕως τοῦ οὐρανοῦ. Dan. 4:21: LXX: ἥξει, Theod.: ἔφθασεν. Dan.

may assume, despite the double Greek terminology, that both times (in Luke 10:9 and 11:20) the Aramaic מטא is at the root (though the Peschitta has קרב in both places), the two passages would still only say: the βασιλεία has come into your very midst; it is already touching you.[17] Without drawing further conclusions from this for the present, we only point out that one cannot base a distinction between the ideas of drawing near and being already present upon alternation of the Greek verbs. Instead, both seem to intertwine: from a certain perspective the same Kingdom is still future which from another is already present.

3. [WAS THE KINGDOM OF GOD PRESENT?]

It is rather generally conceded that the surmise just presented is correct: i.e., that though Jesus generally pictured the Kingdom of God as still future, there are, on the other hand, statements in which the rule of God already appears actualized.[18] And one can probably say that this intertwining of present and future, especially the statements concerning the present, gives dogmatics the right to use the

7:13: LXX: παρῆν, Theod.: ἔφθασεν (in the passage about the Son of man). [For further references, see below, note 17.]

17. [Weiss expands his discussion of these verbs in *Predigt²*, pp. 69–73. Whether Jesus declares the Kingdom present or future depends on his mood at the time. But he normally proclaimed its coming in the future; the sayings in which he speaks proleptically of its presence are the exceptions. See above, pp. 12 f. For references to subsequent studies of these verbs, see Kenneth W. Clark, "Realized Eschatology," *JBL* 59 (1940): 367–83; Werner Georg Kümmel, *Promise and Fulfilment*, trans. D. M. Barton, SBT no. 23 (London: SCM, 1957): 19–25; and Robert Berkey, "ΕΓΓΙΖΕΙΝ, ΦΘΑΝΕΙΝ, and Realized Eschatology," *JBL* 82 (1963): 177–187. Berkey argues on behalf of "realized eschatology," Kümmel against it, except in a restricted sense, and Clark shows that neither verb can mean that the Kingdom has become a matter of present experience.]

18. [Cf. *Predigt²*, pp. 73–88.]

idea of the Kingdom of God as the central concept of the Christian world-view. If originally it were only eschatological or regarded as such, most people today would consider it unsuitable for dogmatics. But one must now face the question: *In what sense* did Jesus speak of a presence of the βασιλεία τοῦ θεοῦ, and is this the sense in which the concept is normally used today?

A number of attempted interpretations must be examined. Probably the most widespread of these interpretations is formulated something like this: "According to Matt. 21:31 (προάγουσιν ὑμᾶς εἰς τὴν βασιλείαν τοῦ θεοῦ) and Matt. 11:11 (ὁ μικρότερος ἐν τῇ βασιλείᾳ τ. οὐρ. μείζων αὐτοῦ = Ἰωάννου ἐστιν), it is evident that there are already some who enter the Kingdom of God, and some who are already in it," namely, "those who see in Jesus the Expected One" (Matt. 11:3,6). They are aready *within* the Kingdom of God. It is conceded, of course, that it is not yet the case that those who believe in the Messiah *compose* or *constitute* the Kingdom of God—"nowhere does Jesus designate the company of his disciples as the Kingdom of God"[19]—but "he brings the rule of God to life, within the community of his adherents (his disciples)."[20] And the latest portrayer of the "Teachings of Jesus" has defined the "Kingdom of God, insofar as it already is realized in the present," as a community of men who are not only in the "right attitude of obedience," but also in full enjoyment of "the Fatherly rule of God."[21]

19. Bernhard Weiss, *Lehrbuch der biblischen Theologie des Neuen Testaments*[5] (Berlin: W. Hertz, 1888), sec. 14, pp. 49–51, [trans. D. Eaton, based on 3rd rev. ed., *Biblical Theology of the New Testament* (Edinburgh: T. & T. Clark, 1882, 1883), 1: 67–70.]

20. Albrecht Ritschl, *Die christliche Lehre von der Rechtfertigung und Versöhnung*[3] (Bonn: A. Marcus, 1889), 2:26–41.

21. Hans Hinrich Wendt, *Die Lehre Jesu* (Göttingen: Vandenhoeck & Ruprecht, 1890), vol. 2, ch. 5. [*The Teaching of Jesus*, trans. John Wilson (New York: Scribner's, n.d.), vol. 2, ch. 5.]

These paraphrasing interpretations of the alleged meaning cannot appeal, as even their proponents concede, to any passage in the Gospels in which the equation of the band of disciples with the Kingdom of God is clearly or plainly made. But that is, after all, a serious drawback. For if Jesus, as is usually assumed, had been so intensely concerned to correct the popular concept of the Kingdom, he would have had to state that concern, if it were to be understood at all, very frequently and emphatically. Surely our evangelists— at least Mark and Matthew—who are moving toward identifying the $\beta\alpha\sigma\iota\lambda\epsilon\acute{\iota}\alpha$ τ. θ. with the contemporary church,[22] would not have let any such saying as this escape them. Moreover, Matthew finds it necessary to introduce not only the concept $\dot{\epsilon}\kappa\kappa\lambda\eta\sigma\acute{\iota}\alpha$, but also the explicit distinction between the present $\beta\alpha\sigma\iota\lambda\epsilon\acute{\iota}\alpha$ τ. $X\rho\iota\sigma\tau\circ\hat{\upsilon}$ and the future heavenly Kingdom.

The passages, furthermore, which are presented by way of evidence for these interpretations likewise give them little support. When it says the tax collectors and prostitutes precede the leaders of the people $\epsilon\dot{\iota}\varsigma$ $\tau\dot{\eta}\nu$ $\beta\alpha\sigma\iota\lambda\epsilon\acute{\iota}\alpha\nu$ τ. θ. [Matt. 21:31], it only means that they are ahead of them on the way that leads to the Kingdom of God: they have a head start; they set a good example. But they are by no means within the Kingdom of God; rather, they are traveling toward it. And the notion that Matt. 11:11 presupposes the possibility that some already may be in the Kingdom of God is proven to be quite the opposite by the next verse:[23]

22. Notice, e.g., how Mark 9:1 seems to contrast the $\beta\alpha\sigma\iota\lambda\epsilon\acute{\iota}\alpha$ $\tau\circ\hat{\upsilon}$ $\theta\epsilon\circ\hat{\upsilon}$ $\dot{\epsilon}\nu$ $\delta\upsilon\nu\acute{\alpha}\mu\epsilon\iota$ (which appears only in our present Mark) as the fulfilled $\beta\alpha\sigma\iota\lambda\epsilon\acute{\iota}\alpha$ of the unfinished earthly one. In this connection, see Romans 1:4, where, with the same addition, this distinction is applied to Christ.
23. [Weiss treats Matt. 11:12 in a separate excursus in *Predigt*[2], pp. 192–197. He maintains that it refers to those who wish to force entrance into the Kingdom (cf. Luke 13:24) or gain possession of it by force (Rom. 10:6). The meaning and authenticity of this verse continue to be disputed. Several writers, e.g., C. H. Dodd and G. E. Ladd, regard it as

ἀπὸ δὲ τῶν ἡμερῶν Ἰωάννου τοῦ βαπτιστοῦ ἕως ἄρτι ἡ βασιλεία τῶν οὐρανῶν βιάζεται καὶ βιασταὶ ἁρπάζουσιν αὐτήν. How these interpreters would like to deduce from this something other than that since the days of John, there has dawned a movement of passionate longing for the Kingdom! Wendt, of course, explains it otherwise:

> Therefore the time of waiting and hoping for the future Kingdom is over; the time of the actualized Kingdom of God, where what matters is to make oneself a member of this Kingdom by energetic resolve, is already at hand.[24]

According to this view, then, Jesus would have described those who had perceived in him the Expected One and had entered "into the Kingdom of God" with a most extraordinary figure: as βιασταὶ ἁρπάζοντες. Is that conceivable? I contend that these words can and must be understood only in the sense of a rebuke. Jesus is describing the kind of people who had been aroused by the Baptist's preaching to the point of impassioned agitation. Jesus rebukes them because they wish to seize by force what they should be waiting for instead. They want to climb up to heaven to haul the Kingdom down (Rom. 10:6). This does fundamental violence to the standpoint of one who fled from the people as soon as he realized ὅτι μέλλουσιν ἔρχεσθαι καὶ ἁρπάζειν αὐτὸν ἵνα ποιήσωσιν βασιλέα (John 6:15). This word of rebuke

evidence for "realized eschatology." Others construe it as anti-Baptist polemic. Another recent theory places it in the context of the early church as an answer to the claim of its persecutors that Jesus wished to seize God-likeness or the rule of heaven for himself: Georg Braumann, "Dem Himmelreich wird Gerwalt angetan," *ZNW* 52 (1961): 104–09. Rudolf Otto thought that it referred to Jesus' followers who press their way into it with all their power and determination: *The Kingdom of God and the Son of Man,* trans. F. V. Filson, B. L. Woolf (London: Lutterworth Press, 1938), pp. 109 ff. For further notes on Matt. 11:11 and 11:12, see R. H. Hiers, *The Kingdom of God in the Synoptic Tradition* (Gainesville, Fla.: Univ. of Florida Press, 1970), pp. 36–42, 57–65.]
24. Wendt, *Lehre Jesu,* 2: 303.

declares, therefore, that there is as yet no Kingdom of God as a community or concrete entity, and that the main fault, which is to be rebuked even in the Baptist and which he had in fact called into being, is impassioned impatience.

From this, however, it follows that the words ὁ μικρό-τερος ἐν τῇ βασιλείᾳ are to be understood hypothetically.[25] In his whole manner, John is so completely foreign to the Kingdom of God that someone, though in other respects much less important, were he even just barely within the Kingdom of God, would far surpass him. To put it another way, just as the relations of rank generally will be reversed in the Kingdom of God, so there John also, if he succeeds in entering it at all,[26] will play a very minor role (precisely

25. Otto Schmoller, *Die Lehre vom Reiche Gottes in den Schriften des Neuen Testaments* (Leiden: E. J. Brill, 1891), p. 40.

26. It is impermissible to press the present tense of ἐστίν for we do not know whether Jesus spoke in the preterite or the future, and whether he used a copula here at all, since we have before us only the view of a translator. It is just as erroneous to draw conclusions from the ἐστίν in Matt. 5:3, 10 (Cf. Wilhelm Baldensperger, *Das Selbstbewusstsein Jesu im Lichte der messianischen Hoffnungen seiner Zeit*[2] (Strassburg: Heitz, 1892), p. 132.) Here the translation is either from an Aramaic future (note the future tense in the adjacent verses), or it is present and means: It is theirs by right, it belongs to them, just as the inheritance belongs to the heir, even though he has not yet come into possession of it. Moreover, there is still the question, with respect to Matthew 11:11 whether ἐν τῇ βασιλείᾳ is to be construed with μικρότερος or with μείζων ἐστίν. [Weiss discusses Matt. 11:11 at greater length in *Predigt*[2], pp. 80–82, and takes the position that the point of the saying lies in the contrast between the present age and the coming age. Even the least important member of the Kingdom then, will be greater than John, the greatest man of the present age, is now. Weiss regards this as an instance of the general reversal of values which Jesus expected in the coming age: "Whoever is great here, will be small there, and vice versa." On this point in general, see *Predigt*[2], pp. 78–88. Weiss's later interpretation is more like that suggested by Schweitzer: John is the greatest natural man of the natural world; but with the dawn of the messianic Kingdom, its members are changed "to a supernatural condition akin to that of the angels" (*Out of My Life and Thought*, p. 8). Cf. below, chapter 9, "The Coming Transformation."]

because of his impatient doubt) as compared with the "little ones" who waited quietly, patiently, and faithfully until the coming of the βασιλεία.

Supporters of the contrary view could draw some further support from certain of the parables, such as the parables of the seed, of the tares, of the grain of mustard seed, and of the leaven. I have no doubt but that our evangelists allegorically explain the field of grain as referring to the contemporary church, the mustard tree as referring to the outwardly visible and expanding Kingdom, and the bread dough as referring to the world which was to be brought to fulfillment by the church. But whether this is the meaning Jesus associated with these parables is far from certain. The two about the mustard seed and the leaven, as is evident from their position after the parable of the sower,[27] certainly intend to describe the fate of the proclaimed word, so that they might be introduced more appropriately with the formula ὅμοιόν ἐστι- τὸ εὐαγγέλιον (or ὁ λόγος). Here again, the introductory formula derived from Mark 4:11 may quite easily mislead us. Behind the parable of the tares, too, as it can be reconstructed from Matthew and Mark,[28] there is the basic idea that an obstructed and seemingly unsuccessful preaching will at last, through God's intervention, have its reward and result. Thus even these passages do not give one the right to identify the Kingdom of God in any sense with the group of disciples, or to think of it as being actualized in them. From this it also follows that one cannot expound Luke 17:21 in that sense either. When Jesus says here that the βασιλεία τοῦ θεοῦ is already in the midst of the Pharisees, this does not give any occasion for seeing here an allusion to the actualization of the Kingdom of God within the group of disciples. On the contrary, such

27. Cf. *Studien und Kritiken*, 1891, p. 318. (See above, n. 9.)
28. B. Weiss, *Lehrbuch*, pp. 159 ff.

a meaning is improbable, since Jesus' words, in some way or other, contain a paradox. For they can only be understood to mean that *without* the Pharisees' observing it, the βασιλεία has been realized in some mysterious manner. Therefore, it refers neither to the gathering of a group of disciples, nor even to the establishment of a new righteousness, but to mysterious events, which are invisible to the perverse eye. More will be said below as to what Jesus meant here.

What speaks more forcefully than all else against the kind of interpretation to which we have been objecting is the fact that Jesus put in the mouths of his disciples, as the *first* petition of their prayer,[29] the words: ἐλθέτω ἡ βασιλεία σου. Let us be careful lest somehow or other we play down this fact and these words. The meaning is not "may thy Kingdom grow," "may thy Kingdom be perfected," but rather, "may thy Kingdom *come.*" *For the disciples,* the βασιλεία is not yet here, not even in its beginnings; therefore Jesus bids them: ζητεῖτε τὴν βασιλείαν (Luke 12:31). This yearning and longing for its coming, this ardent prayer for it, and the constant hope that it will come— that it will come soon—this is their religion. We would import an opaque and confusing element into this unified and clearly unambiguous religious frame of mind were we to think somehow of a "coming in an ever higher degree" or of a growth or increase of the Kingdom. Just as there can be no different stages of its being—without prejudice to what Harnack has explained concerning its preexistence[30] —so likewise there are no stages of its coming. Either the βασιλεία is here, or it is not yet here. For the disciples and

29. The words ἁγιασθήτω τὸ ὄνομά σου comprise only a reverent, liturgical introductory formula.
30. Adolf von Harnack, *Dogmengeschichte²* (Freiburg: Mohr [Siebeck], 1888–1890), 1: 710 ff. (Trans. N. Buchanon, *History of Dogma* (Boston: Little, Brown & Co., 1902), 2: 318 ff.)

for the early church it is not yet here. And when Jesus calls them blessed because of what they see and hear (Matt. 13:17), the fact that glorious prophecies have been fulfilled in their presence is surely sufficient basis for this declaration—but the one great and foremost promise still remains to be fulfilled.

4. [JESUS' WARFARE AGAINST SATAN'S KINGDOM]

In what sense, then, does Jesus speak of a "presence" of the Kingdom of God? To put it superficially, one might say: in a paradoxical way.[31] Certainly the two principal passages, Matt: 12:28 and Luke 17:21, are spoken in rejoinder to opponents who dismiss its presence. But this answer is insufficient. What seems paradoxical to us is not so at all from Jesus' standpoint; for him it is the most compelling reality! We have to bear in mind that for the Israelites, and likewise for Jesus, there existed a twofold world, and thus also a twofold occurrence of events. The world of men and history is only the lower floor of the world's structure. The world of the angels and spirits is erected above that. Both parts make up the κόσμος (1 Cor. 4:9). Moreover, what happens on earth has its exact parallel in heaven. All history is only the consequence, effect, or parallel copy of heavenly events. Thus an event which on earth is only just beginning to take place may not merely be already determined, but even already enacted in heaven.[32] A classical example of this is Rev. 12:7 ff. Satan, in the form of the dragon, is cast down from heaven by Michael and his

31. [Cf. *Predigt²*, pp. 88–95.]
32. [So also Paul Volz, *Die Eschatologie der jüdischen Gemeinde*, 2nd ed. (Tübingen: Mohr [Siebeck], 1934), p. 7, and Otto Betz, "The Kerygma of Luke," *Interpretation* 22 (1968): 135 ff.]

angels, whereupon the heavenly hosts begin to sing the song of triumph: ἄρτι ἐγένετο ἡ σωτηρία καὶ ἡ δύναμις καὶ ἡ βασιλεία τοῦ θεοῦ ἡμῶν ... ὅτι ἐβλήθην ὁ κατήγωρ τῶν ἀδελφῶν ἡμῶν (Rev. 12:10). Through the fall of Satan, God's rule is won in a fully real sense. Yet the βασιλεία τοῦ θεοῦ is still in no way realized on earth. Here the struggle is just beginning. One who sees this, however, can observe this struggle with equanimity, for Satan is already overthrown, his power is broken and gradually will be overcome on earth, as well.

A further example: for Paul, sin in the flesh is condemned by the death of Christ (Rom. 8:3) because the σῶμα τῆς ἁμαρτίας is destroyed (Rom. 6:6). Not just the σάρξ of Christ, but σάρξ everywhere—this great collective substance which in Paul's thought is no vague idea, but a living, powerful entity—this σάρξ is put to death, it is robbed of its might, and therefore the Christians are dead (Col. 3:3), their σάρξ no longer exists. We are constantly tempted to employ certain vague phrases—e.g., "so to say," "as it were," "basically," "the idea is," "in principle" —in order to play down these thoughts which were understood quite seriously and realistically. That is not our privilege, however, for to Paul these are not metaphors but facts.[33] To be sure, they are facts which are invisible to the unperceiving eye, but the believer is as firmly convinced of them as he is of his own existence, facts which were settled and established once for all time in the great battle with the spirits, when Christ (or God) ἀπεξεδύσατο τὰς ἀρχὰς καὶ τὰς ἐξουσίας καὶ ἐδειγμάτισεν ἐν παρρησίᾳ (Col. 2:15). But while these realities have transpired in the realm between heaven and earth, they must now be fought

33. [Cf. Rudolf Bultmann's ambiguous interpretation of such terms as "figurative, rhetorical language" in his *Theology of the New Testament*, trans. Kendrick Grobel (New York: Scribner's, 1954), 1: 244 f.]

out on earth. Therefore, although Christians are already dead, although the great world power σάρξ has already received the deathblow, it is nevertheless necessary to struggle against it as if it were still alive. Its πράξεις are still here and demand watchfulness and endurance. Here, too, one sees this parallelism of events—this distinction between what is happening on stage, and the decisive major events off stage.[34]

In this light we understand the problematic sayings and views of Jesus under consideration here.[35] It has recently been shown how in the Gospel of Luke, Jesus' whole life is regarded as a struggle on the part of the bearer of the Spirit of God against the kingdom of Satan.[36] The evangelist's basic idea here rests upon unquestionably authentic utterances of Jesus. He is conscious of carrying on a struggle against the Satanic kingdom. This is to be seen most clearly in the exorcisms. Jesus naturally shared the view that demoniacs were actually possessed by spirits. And when, through the impact of his powerful personality, through the upsurge of fear and confidence which he aroused in the sick, he freed them from their demonic ty-

34. Cf. the relation of the Prologue of the Gospel of John to the Gospel itself.

35. [Viz. Matt. 12:28; Luke 17:21.]

36. Colin Campbell, *Critical Studies in St. Luke's Gospel* (Edinburgh and London: W. Blackwood & Sons, 1891). [That *Luke* connects the Spirit with exorcism has since been disputed: Eduard Schweizer, et al., *Spirit of God* (London: A. & C. Black, 1960), esp. pp. 24–45; John Edmund Yates, *The Spirit and the Kingdom* (London: SPCK, 1963), pp. 90 ff. *Mark* does make this connection, as James M. Robinson has ably demonstrated in *The Problem of History in Mark* (Naperville: Allenson, 1957). See also Howard C. Kee, "The Terminology of Mark's Exorcism Stories," *NTS* 14 (1968): 232-46, which lends substantial support to Weiss's theory that through exorcising demons Jesus was preparing for the coming of the Kingdom of God (See above, pp. 42 f., n. 118). Thus also Otto Betz, "Jesu heiliger Krieg," *NT* 2 (1958): 116–37, and Hiers, *Kingdom of God*, pp. 30–56.]

rants, he knew that he was doing decisive damage to the well-organized kingdom of Satan. He was taking ever vaster provinces of this kingdom away from the rule of the Prince of this world. Accordingly, what could be observed outwardly in his success in healing, what amazed his friends and aroused the suspicions of his enemies, all referred back to great decisive events in the kingdom of the Spirits. To Jesus, every visible healing signified an invisible, yet no less certain, defeat for the "Enemy."

This meaning comes out in that very important dispute with his adversaries when they charged him with being in league with Beelzebul. Here he showed how absurd it was of them to suppose an alliance with Beelzebul for the destruction of Satan's kingdom (Matt. 12:25–27), and that instead, they ought ($ἄρα$) to draw the conclusion from his successful exorcisms that the kingly rule of God was already begun. Certainly this fact was not an obvious one, and would have been admitted least of all by his opponents, but in Jesus' prophetic consciousness it was incontrovertible. To be sure, the Pharisees were unaccustomed to the idea that the establishment of the Kingdom would proceed from God's side so quietly, so gradually, and moving from the inward to the outward. For this reason they would have understood this saying of Jesus no better than they did the other, Luke 17:21. Jesus' answer evidently struck them as startling. *Therefore Jesus asserts something here which generally he does not presuppose elsewhere:* that the $βασιλεία$ is already here in some invisible fashion.[37] He clearly wishes to impress upon the minds of his malevolent questioners how, though they have eyes, they do not see. What is taking place in their midst—how on all sides the power of the devil is being defeated and consequently (because of the utter opposition between the $βασιλεία$ $τοῦ$ $θεοῦ$ and

37. As to $οὐ$ $μετὰ$ $παρατηρήσεως$, see below, pp. 89–91.

the βασιλεία τοῦ σατανᾶ) the rule of God is already beginning—escapes them completely. In these two sayings, Jesus stressed a side of the matter which usually is not emphasized elsewhere. Although they normally thought only about the glorious external establishment of the messianic Kingdom, what is described here is the altogether supranatural and superhistorical establishment of the power of God over Satan, to whom for a while the world had been subjected [Luke 4:6].

The disciples too, according to Luke 10:9, were to awaken the people to this realization, at least if we have been correct in equating ἤγγικεν with ἔφθασεν. This also would have been the content of the preaching in Nazareth (Luke 4:17), and possibly even that of the κήρυγμα in Mark 1:14. Therefore, if Jesus already speaks of a Kingdom of God which is present, it is not because there is present a community of disciples among whom God's will is done, as if God's rule were realized from the side of men. Rather, Jesus does so because by his own activity the power of Satan, who above all others is the source of evil, is being broken.[38] But these are moments of sublime prophetic enthusiasm, when an awareness of victory comes over him. It is noteworthy that these expressions are uttered in a context of fiercely hostile attack, and in response to scoffing

38. With this opposition between βασιλεία τοῦ θεοῦ and βασιλεία τοῦ σατανᾶ, cf. *Assumption of Moses* 10:2, which aptly illustrates the meaning as understood by Jesus and his contemporaries. [See P. Volz, *Eschatologie*, pp. 86–89, regarding the "Kingdom of Satan" in Jewish literature. Volz calls attention especially to *Testament of Daniel* 5 and 6. See also Walter Grundmann, *Der Begriff der Kraft in der neutestamentlichen Gedankenwelt* (Stuttgart: W. Kohlhammer, 1932), esp. pp. 46–74. Both Volz and Grundmann substantiate Weiss's contention that Jesus, and the early Christians generally, shared the cosmic dualism of their Jewish contemporaries. The Qumran literature, notably the *War Scroll*, gives further evidence concerning the contemporary concept. See Herbert G. May, "Cosmological References in the Qumran Doctrine of the Two Spirits and in Old Testament Imagery," *JBL* 82 (1963): 1–14.]

questions (Luke 17:20; [Matt. 12:24]). In such moments it may have become clear to Jesus that he knew and saw more than did these dull observers who still refused to notice any change in the course of the world (Luke 12:54 ff.).

Alongside such expressions as these, however, stands a great profusion of sayings in which the establishment of the Kingdom remains reserved for the future, whether near or distant. This relationship between these two types of sayings is to be explained by reference to the parallelism implicit in the religious viewpoint mentioned above: Satan's kingdom is already broken, the rule of God is already gaining ground; but it has not yet become a historical event. The Kingdom of God, in the form that Jesus expected it, is not yet established on earth.

5. [WAS JESUS THE "FOUNDER" OF THE KINGDOM OF GOD?]

Along with the interpretation which has just been rejected, there is another one related to it which might also be discussed here briefly, although the question will be treated more fully below [pp. 81–83]. The recent dogmatic interpretation of the concept βασιλεία τοῦ θεοῦ speaks unhesitatingly of Jesus as the "Founder" and "Establisher" of the Kingdom of God, without bothering to inquire whether this use of the term reflects Jesus' understanding or ours instead. Though in retrospect *we* certainly can say as a judgment of faith that Jesus established the Kingdom of God within his church, it is just as certain that such a conception or expression is far-removed from the sphere of Jesus' ideas.

Aside from Matt. 16:17 f., there is no reliably attested saying of Jesus in which he designates himself as founder of God's Kingdom. He is the sower, who scatters the seed of the Word in men's hearts, but all this is only preparatory, for he never says that it is his task ἀποκαθιστάναι τὴν βασιλείαν τῷ Ἰσραήλ. Such an idea is altogether impossible from the standpoint of Jesus' outlook as a whole, as we shall see when we attempt to answer the more far-reaching question: What role did Jesus assign to himself with respect to the establishment of the Kingdom of God, and within that Kingdom? Only in one respect is Jesus more important than the sower or a mere preparer: he prepares the way for the Kingdom of God in that he is successfully engaged in driving the present imperious Ruler of αἰὼν οὗτος, Satan, from his position of lordship. Indeed, according to Luke 10:18 ff., the real, superhistorical basis for all the success of Jesus and his disciples is the fact that Satan has fallen. Previously he had held a position in heaven as one among the other angels of God; indeed, the present world had been handed over to him by God (Luke 4:6) for him to rule and enslave. Now he has fallen from heaven, and thereby the backbone of his dominion is broken. Thus it is to be understood that his agents, the demons, also are no longer in a position to offer any resistance to the powerful command of Jesus or even to the mere naming of his feared name.

Jesus was convinced (ἐθεώρουν), whether in a vision of the sort that he had experienced at his baptism and temptation, or in some moment of inner assurance,[39] that such was the case. Usually this θεωρεῖν is presumed to have taken place sometime during the absence of the seventy (Luke 10:1–16),[40] but this interpretation is arbitrary since Jesus'

39. [In *Predigt²*, pp. 92 f., Weiss also cites the transfiguration (Mark 9:2 ff.) and the "analogous experience" described in John 12:31a: "The result is the unshakable certainty that the power of Satan is done with, and the Kingdom of God has dawned (*angebrochen*)."]
40. E.g., Wendt, *Lehre Jesu*, 2: 301 f.

own earlier success presupposes the fall of Satan (Luke 11:21 f.). It is necessary, then, to look for some earlier occasion. The "victory over the strong one" [Mark 3:27 and parallels] has been regarded quite correctly by many as an allusion to the temptation. However one may interpret this, the substance of the reports in the Gospels must somehow or other be derived from sayings of Jesus to the effect that at the beginning of his activity he had overcome Satan, so that the δύναμις of the Adversary is under control and can no longer harm him or his followers (Luke 10:17 ff.; 22:31 f.).[41] How we ourselves are to think of this struggle can only be conjectured—what alone matters is the result of the struggle as it later lived on in Jesus' consciousness. There can be no objection to speaking of Jesus as "Founder of the Kingdom of God" if one is willing to think of it in these terms just described—that is, if one keeps in view the destruction of the kingdom of Satan (1 John 3:8). I imagine, however, that most people will neither be satisfied with this more negative description of the concept, nor want to understand it in this completely supranaturalistic way of looking at things, which is mythological from our standpoint.

6. [JESUS' ROLE IN THE ESTABLISHMENT OF THE KINGDOM]

It is important at this point, however, to raise, at least in a preliminary way, the question as to how Jesus related himself to the establishment of the Kingdom of God. What role did he assign to himself in connection with its coming? It cannot be stressed too emphatically that, according to the testimony of the Gospels, and on grounds of internal probability, *the* activity of Jesus, besides overcoming Sa-

41. [See above, however, pp. 42 f., n. 118.]

tan's kingdom, seems to have consisted in εὐαγγελίζεσθαι, announcing the coming of the Kingdom of God. It must be emphasized, moreover, that in principle this activity is not basically different from that of the Baptist. What is referred to here is not Jesus' baptizing (John 3:25; 4:1 ff.), but rather his call to repentance and announcement of the nearness of the Kingdom, which are unanimously attested by the synoptic Gospels. I do not see how this activity is to be construed as "properly messianic," while the Baptist's is considered preparatory. Both, in fact, are exactly the same. Indeed, one may say: Precisely from *Jesus' own standpoint,* his entire activity is *not* of messianic, but of preparatory character. It is evident from a great number of passages that Jesus thinks the establishment of the βασιλεία τοῦ θεοῦ will be mediated solely by God's supernatural intervention. Any human activity in connection with it thus is ruled out completely. Even though the "Son of man" is assigned a prominent role in this connection, we shall see later on that the predicate "Son of man" is always associated in Jesus' self-consciousness with the idea of an "exaltation" (John 3:14). Thus, since Jesus is now a rabbi, a prophet, he has nothing in common with the Son of man, except the claim that he will *become* the Son of man.[42] Thus even he cannot intervene in the development of the Kingdom of God. He has to wait, just as the people have to wait,

42. [Weiss maintains and develops this interpretation of Jesus' "messianic self-consciousness" below, pp. 115 ff., and in *Predigt²*, pp. 154 ff., 166, 175, and *Earliest Christianity* (New York: Harper, 1959), 2: 733. Jesus did not regard himself as the Christ during his earthly ministry. Neither did the early church so regard him. But Jesus believed that he would become the Messiah, and the early church expected him to come as such. In this connection, see John A. T. Robinson, "The Most Primitive Christology of All?", in *Twelve New Testament Studies*, SBT no. 34 (London: SCM, 1962): 139–153. But also Reginald H. Fuller, *The Foundations of New Testament Christology* (New York: Scribner's, 1965) esp. pp. 158–62.]

until God once again definitively takes up the rule. Since he himself is averse to every revolutionary movement, and as long as God has not yet intervened, he is willing to render unto Caesar what is Caesar's (Mark 12:17). In the same way, he flees when men want to make him King (John 6:15), and in his eyes the βιασταί, who wish to force the coming of the Kingdom (Matt. 11:12), commit the greatest offense. They are irreligious. Certainly one is to seek the βασιλεία, but only by preparing oneself and acquiring the righteousness which God commends (Matt. 6:33, 5:20). One is to strive to press in through the narrow gate (Luke 13:24), but not to be anxious for the morrow (Matt. 6:34). And however much one may long for the days of the Son of man, it profits nothing (Luke 17:22). The Kingdom does not on that account come any more quickly, for the Father has reserved the time and the hour to his own authority (Acts 1:7). Not even the Son and the angels know it (Mark 13:32), to say nothing of being able to do anything about it. For mankind, and thus for Jesus also, this means: Pray that the Kingdom may come, and trust that it will come. It is promised to the little flock; therefore God will vindicate and redeem his elect (Luke 12:32; 18:7; 21:28).

7. [JESUS' EXPECTATION AT THE LAST SUPPER (Luke 22:14–30)]

This, then, is the situation: Even if in isolated moments of exaltation the Master glimpsed the secret progress of the rule of God, Jesus' attitude in general is the same as that which he assumed his disciples shared, namely: May the Kingdom of God come, and the kingdom of Satan pass away. Or, as the *Didache* (10:6) expresses it, may grace come and the world pass away! Jesus' words at the Last

Supper show how little he thought of himself as leaving the "Kingdom of God" behind in the form of his group of disciples: he will not again drink of the fruit of the vine until the Kingdom of God has come (Luke 22:18). Then and there he will drink it "anew." Is stronger proof needed to show that Jesus parted from this life with the painful realization that the Kingdom of God, which he had proclaimed to be so near, still had not been established?

Another farewell saying reported by Luke at the Last Supper (Luke 22:28 ff.) expresses this sadly: as his bequest to his faithful followers, he leaves the βασιλεία which his Father had made over to *him* in a διαθήκη, i.e., a contractual promise. This βασιλεία consists in their ruling over the twelve tribes. Jesus had as yet experienced none of this rule himself. His βασιλεία, bequeathed to him by God, which he now left behind to his disciples, was an invisible crown, a spiritual claim to the rule. More than this claim, this blessed hope, he could not bequeath even to his own, for how were they to ascend to the "twelve thrones" when he, himself, their spiritually more powerful Master, had been obliged to wait in patience? It is unnecessary to list other passages in addition to these; they could only detract from this intrinsically convincing mood.[43]

8. [WHEN DID JESUS EXPECT THE KINGDOM TO COME?]

We now ask somewhat more precisely: When and how did Jesus think the actualization of the Kingdom of God would take place? What will be the blessings that it brings? What are the conditions for participation in it? And, final-

---

43. [A futuristic interpretation of Jesus' expectation at the Last Supper is presented also by Joachim Jeremias, *The Eucharistic Words of Jesus,* trans. N. Perrin, rev. ed. (New York: Scribner's, 1966).]

ly, what will be the place of Jesus himself in this King-dom?[44]

First of all, when did he expect the establishment of the Kingdom to occur? The words of farewell mentioned just above, according to which this is to take place only after his death, cannot by themselves provide an answer to this question. For the question arises whether Jesus was always so resigned to this view, or whether there had not been mo-ments when he hoped that he might yet live to see that great event. We have no direct utterances from Jesus on this, unless one chooses to regard $\mathring{\eta}\gamma\gamma\iota\kappa\epsilon\nu$, in the sense dis-cussed above, as implying a quite imminent establishment of the Kingdom. But we may infer indirectly that at some earlier period in his ministry Jesus believed the coming of the Kingdom closer than turned out later to be the case. Otherwise, how is one to interpret the fact that already during his lifetime he sent his disciples on a mission through the land of the Jews? To speak of a trial or practice mission does not seem to me permissible. What could be the use of any testing or apprenticeship if it was not carried out under the eye of the Master? Rather, the sending out of the twelve has very much the character of a *supporting mission*. Its purpose was to multiply the preaching about the coming Kingdom, to scatter abroad the seed of the word over larger fields than *one* sower alone could reach. But how is such a mission to be accounted for, other than on the supposition that *speed* above all was essential, that no time be lost? Moreover, what the fact of the mission of the disciples it-self teaches us is expressed still more clearly in certain of the instructions to the disciples. The disciples were admon-ished (Matt. 10:14; Luke 10:10) that in case a town should not receive them, they were immediately and em-phatically to abandon all further attempts to approach it

44. [Cf. *Predigt²*, pp. 100–105.]

and shake off its dust from their feet. Such procedure is anything but "pastoral," and certainly does not correspond to what we would expect from a preacher of the Gospel. It can only be explained on the supposition that no time may be lost with fruitless or problematical efforts. Where they meet with unresponsiveness, no more energy dare be wasted there which might better be directed toward receptive souls. The expectation of the *immediate* onset of the end forms the background for these ideas.[45]

But under the pressure of certain circumstances,[46] Jesus became convinced that the end had been postponed. That which was so eagerly awaited was not yet happening, and to one who looked more deeply, it was apparent that the Kingdom *could* not yet come. To date, the people had not yet brought forth in their ethical behavior the mature fruit of a genuine μετάνοια. To be sure, a messianic-revolutionary movement had broken out, but this is precisely what Jesus had to condemn (Matt. 11:11 f.). In general, however, things had remained pretty much as they were. The people still wandered about like sheep without a shepherd. The Word of Jesus and his messengers had borne fruit only in a small number of hearts. Most of the seed had been lost immediately in indifference, thoughtlessness, and in the cares and pleasures of life. But what was worse, the leaders of the people explicitly rejected the purpose of God (Luke 7:30); they opposed Jesus and blasphemed the Spirit which was working in him. They thus committed an un-

---

45. [This kind of interpretation of the "missionary instructions" has also been supported by Dom Jacques Dupont, " 'Vous n'aurez pas achevé les villes d' Israel avant que le fils de l'homme ne vienne'," *NT* 2 (1958): 228–244. See also Hiers, *Kingdom of God,* pp. 66–71.]

46. [What Weiss means here appears more clearly in *Predigt²,* pp. 101 f., where he says that at some point in Jesus' ministry, he became certain that the end, because of the lack of repentance by the people, had been delayed. See above, pp. 9 f.]

forgivable sin and therefore are excluded from the Kingdom of God. Thus the threat of the prophet *Enoch* (98:9 f.) can be applied to the whole people, the leaders as well as those whom they misled:

> Woe to you, you fools, for through your folly you shall perish; and as you do not give heed to the wise, so nothing good will be yours. And now, know that you are prepared for the day of destruction, and do not hope, you sinners, that you will live; instead you shall depart and die, *for there is no ransom for you;* for you are prepared for the day of the great judgment, and for the day of tribulation and great shame for your spirit.

Even more startling is the fact that it turns out that the sons of the Kingdom, those to whom the βασιλεία belongs as the inheritance belongs to its heir, must be cast into outer darkness (Matt. 8:12), and that the Kingdom must be taken from them (Matt. 21:43 f.)[47] unless some special deliverance occurs. Both from this line of thought and from pondering the relentless enmity of his opponents, Jesus concluded that the establishment by God of the messianic Kingdom could not yet take place; that an enormous obstacle, the guilt of the people, had to be removed; and that he would not live to see this happen, but first must fall victim to the hatred of his opponents. But from Jesus' religious understanding of his whole life, this could not mean the failure of his work. It must rather be a means for bringing about the final goal. And since the sin which will cause his death is at the same time the chief obstacle to the coming of the Kingdom, he seized upon the audacious and paradoxical

47. [The latter saying (Matt. 21:43) appears only in the First Gospel. Many critics now consider it secondary: e.g., Ernst Lohmeyer, *Das Evangelium des Matthäus*, ed. Werner Schmauch (Göttingen: Vandenhoeck & Ruprecht, 1956), pp. 314 f. Some think it may be dominical, but not originally in the present context: e.g., Floyd V. Filson, *The Gospel According to St. Matthew* (New York: Harper, 1961), p. 229.]

idea—or the idea seized him—that his death itself should be the ransom for the people otherwise destined to destruction (Mark 10:45). He must give up his life ὑπὲρ πολλῶν as a λύτρον, which the many, the people themselves, could not offer.

Ordinarily, the "many" on whose behalf Jesus offers up his life is interpreted to mean the followers and disciples of Jesus. But why would they need a ransom? Had he not promised them upon their repentance the sure possession of the Kingdom? Had he not inspired them, as he had the paralytic and the woman apprehended in adultery, with the certainty that their sins were forgiven and thus formed no obstacle to their entrance into the Kingdom? And, even the words at the Last Supper (according to the synoptic tradition represented by Mark) still say only that as the bread is broken and the wine poured out, so also must his body be killed and his blood flow ὑπὲρ πολλῶν (Mark 14:24). Jesus does not say what would have been so easy to say if that had been his meaning: ὑπὲρ ὑμῶν, "for you." That reading first appears in Paul (1 Cor. 11:24 f.) and in the non-genuine words in Luke 22:19b–20, which are missing[48] in [Codex] D and it⁴, and in any case are influenced by Paulinism.

At the same time, this is admittedly spoken from the viewpoint of covenant sacrifice, which naturally benefits all members of the covenant, but, nevertheless, Jesus' death is first of all the sin offering for the people.[49] Because Jesus'

48. Brooke Foss Westcott and Fenton John Anthony Hort, *The New Testament in the Original Greek* (Cambridge and London: Macmillan, 1895), vol. 2, app. 63.

49. Only such an interpretation as this can explain how it is that there is no mention of the saving significance of Christ's death *for the church* in the earliest Jewish-Christian community. (The documents of this community, in my judgment, include only the Epistle of James and the sources of the Gospels—the Logia and the "Ebionite source of Luke"—but not 1 Peter.) Only in this way is it comprehensible that a completely

unavoidable death is thus inserted into the chain of divine Salvation-decrees [*Heilsratschlüsse*], a further conclusion is apparent. His death is only something preliminary, a transitional stage to a heavenly existence with the Father, where he will be installed in heavenly splendor.[50] This state of exaltation, also, is not permanent, but needs continue only until the repentance which Jesus was unable to obtain from the people—until the reformation which the Baptist initiated, and which Jesus carried forward but left unfinished—is brought to completion through the preaching of repentance by his followers (Acts 3:19 ff.). After that, he will come again with all the magnificence and splendor that had been expected of the Messiah since the days of Daniel.

When will that be? When is the Kingdom of God coming? So ask the Pharisees, half curiously, half in ridicule (Luke 17:20 f.). Jesus' answer is difficult to interpret, for the words οὐ μετὰ παρατηρήσεως seem at first glance to constitute a more precise definition of ἔρχεται: One accordingly expects some kind of characterization of the Kingdom of God itself, or of the manner of its coming. From this feeling arises the interpretation still represented by Weizsäcker

different viewpoint with regard to the Last Supper from Paul's is still to be found in the *Didache* (10).

50. It is incomprehensible to me how Wendt (*Lehre Jesu*, 2: 542 ff. [Hans Hinrich Wendt, *Die Lehre Jesu* (Göttingen, 1886), trans. J. Wilson, *The Teaching of Jesus* (Edinburgh: T. & T. Clark, 1892), 2: 265 ff.]) can say that Jesus' certainty of his resurrection is no proof of his special messianic self-consciousness, but rather that he only applied to himself the same idea of the resurrection which he preached to his followers. Such a view ignores the basic difference between the raising of Jesus and that of his disciples, which is that the latter, if they die *prior* to the coming of the Kingdom, will be raised at the messianic *judgment,* whereas Jesus will depart from Hades *at once.* To be sure, the Ebionite source of Luke, which seems to have modified essentially the idea of the Kingdom of God (Luke 23:43), assumed a direct entrance into heaven for the faithful also, but this is scarcely what Jesus meant. [Weiss seems to have changed his mind about this point later. See below, n. 100.]

and Wendt: not with ostentatious display, which is essentially the same as Luther's; not with outward manifestations. But the word παρατήρησις can mean nothing of the kind. After all, to adhere to the literal meaning of the word, the παρατήρησις takes place on the side of the waiting people. This is indeed surprising, but Luke 9:39 illustrates the same grammatical usage: καὶ ἰδοὺ πνεῦμα λαμβάνει αὐτὸν καὶ ἐξαίφνης κράζει καὶ σπαράσσει αὐτὸν μετὰ ἀφροῦ. Here, likewise, μετὰ ἀφροῦ refers to an attendant circumstance which, strictly speaking, characterizes not the afflicting demon, but the afflicted invalid. So, too, in the passage in question, Luke 17:20 f. Here all that is said is that the Kingdom of God does not come in such a way that one can observe its coming by means of certain signs. Usually it is assumed that all outward events in connection with the coming of the Kingdom of God are here repudiated, so that it comes only in an "inward" manner. But this is impossible if one considers Jesus' outlook as a whole. For example, as we will see, the entire old world will break up with the coming of the Kingdom. Does not this imply outward events? The word παρατήρησις is borrowed from astronomical terminology, where it is used, for instance, in speaking of the observation of certain signs by which one detects an imminent heavenly event, such as a solar eclipse. It is used in this sense here, also. It constitutes a pronouncement against the method of the apocalyptist. The apocalyptist feels that by combining prophecies and deciphering the signs of the times he is able to determine from παρατήρησις how long it will be *until* the Kingdom of God comes. Jesus rejects this whole procedure, as the following discourse (Luke 17:21 ff.) shows. One cannot observe its coming in advance. One cannot say: Look here! Look there! See, there are the decisive signs! To illustrate how false this whole method is, he cites the fact that despite all their calculations and combinations it has escaped the Pharisees that the decisive beginnings of the rule of God are already present in their midst. And now Jesus shows how suddenly and surprisingly the coming of the Son of man will take shape, overthrowing all speculations. This difficult saying, therefore, is parallel in substance to that of Mark 13:32: "But of that day or that hour no one knows, not even the angels in heaven, nor the Son, but only the Father." This is a matter of religious principle. So long as the time of the end can somehow be calculated, the establishment of the Kingdom remains a human work. But for Jesus it is unqualifiedly the work of God, and therefore to be left to God in every respect.[51]

Moreover, he regarded another matter as thoroughly settled. Whatever uncertainty there may be as to the exact time of the Second Coming, it is only conceivable within the lifetime of the generation among which Jesus worked. This does not contradict what has been said before. The end is to occur sometime within the important period of the next ten, twenty, or thirty years; it should not be stated any more precisely than this. This positing of a *terminus post quem non,* however, is not based at all on combination and calculation, but is an immediate intuitive religious certainty.

51. Part of the interpretation which I set forth in *Studien und Kritiken,* 1892, pp. 247 f. (see below, n. 53), is marked by a lack of clarity which I hope may be overcome in the discussion above. I owe this clarification substantially to a conversation with Professor Dr. Leo in Göttingen. [Weiss develops this interpretation somewhat more fully in *Predigt²,* pp. 85–88. There he suggests that Luke 17:20a is a "trick question" by which the Pharisees tried to trap Jesus. They wanted him to state when the Kingdom would come, so that when it failed to do so, they could then expose him as a fraud. For further discussion of Luke 17:20–21, see Hiers, *Kingdom of God,* pp. 22–29. Jacques Winandy, O.S.B., interprets Mark 13:32 basically as Weiss does here: "Le Logion de l'Ignorance," *Revue Biblique* 75 (1968): 63–79.]

It means that Jesus will carry forward his work with these men with whom he had begun it, that he must make good his word to them in good things as in evil, and that he will make things clear between them and himself. It is only natural and human in this regard that Jesus was not thinking about his return at some distant time, but about the men for whom he lived, suffered, and died. Therefore, he will remain away long enough to leave the people ample time for repentance and regeneration [Cf. 2 Pet. 3:9]. In these terms we can see how the postponement of the end and the different statements concerning it may be rendered intelligible.

9. [THE COMING TRANSFORMATION]

We now ask *how* Jesus conceived of the events related to God's establishment of the Kingdom.[52] The parousia speech in Luke 17 [vv. 22 ff.] brings up a number of points. First of all, the establishment of the Kingdom will not be accomplished somewhere in a corner; rather, just as lightning flashes across the whole sky, visible to all, so too will the appearance of the Son of man take place before the whole world. It will then be comparable to the deluge in the time of Noah. Certainly the suddenness of its coming is the main point of the comparison, but its universality and destructiveness are also important. That it is a matter of a world-wide event is also evidenced by the other parousia saying which can be sifted out of Mark 13.[53] It begins with wars and insurrection, but the decisive signs are enumerated in Mark 13:24–25a. It is described exactly in the sixth chapter of Revelation: The sun will be darkened, the moon will no longer give its light, and the stars will fall from the

52. [Cf. *Predigt²*, pp. 105–111.]
53. Cf. "Die Komposition der synoptischen Wiederkunftsrede," *Studien und Kritiken*, 1892, pp. 246–270.

heavens. The answer to the disciples' question in Mark 13:4 f., is found in verse 29: ὅταν ἴδητε ταῦτα γινόμενα γινώσκετε ὅτι ἐγγύς ἐστιν ἐπὶ θύραις. What is pictured in these words is neither more nor less than what is drawn in rather more dramatic colors in Rev. 6:12–17: the breakup of the old world which will bury even the temple in its ruins [Mark 13:2]. Naturally, we should avoid at the outset any kind of reformulation of this idea, however strange it may seem to us. As it now stands, it expresses what the early Christians meant: This old world cannot assimilate the Kingdom of God, the αἰὼν μέλλων; everything must become new (Rev. 21:1, 5; 2 Pet. 3:10). The Jewish author of 4 Ezra had already expressed the standard idea:

> . . . the age is hastening swiftly to its end. For it will not be able to bring the things that have been promised to the righteous in their appointed times, because this age is full of sadness and infirmities. For the evil . . . has been sown. . . . If therefore . . . the place where the evil has been sown does not pass away, the field where the good has been sown will not come.[54]

This event of a new creation and transformation of the world is most clearly intimated by Jesus in the word παλιγγενεσία (Matt. 19:28). Jesus, too, seems to have expected a new heaven and a new earth. In any case, he declared that he would drink of the fruit of the vine *anew* in the Kingdom of God his Father (Mark 14:25). And the land which will produce this never-withering vine is the promised land, arising in new splendor. When the Kingdom of God has come, this land will no longer be a parade ground for for-

54. 4 Ezra [2 Esdras] 4:26 ff. [The passage cited here is taken from the RSV Apocrypha; the Latin text given by Weiss reads as follows: *festinans festinat saeculum pertransire; non capiet portare quae in temporibus justis repromissa sunt, quoniam plenum maestitia est saeculum hoc et infirmatibus. Seminatum est enim malum; . . . si ergo . . . non discesserit locus ubi seminatum est malum, non veniat* (=*veniet* οὐ μὴ ἔλθῃ) *ager, ubi seminatum est bonum.*]

eign armies or a colony for exploitation by fortune-seeking rulers, but the sole possession of the πραεῖς, the meek who ardently long for it but *now* are pariahs in this land which, by divine right, is theirs. But even the peoples who are to live in this Kingdom must also participate in that transformation. If they are to see God (Matt. 5:8), if they are to enjoy the treasures which are insusceptible to rust and moths (Matt. 6:19 f.), if they wish to sit at the heavenly banquet, then naturally they may not bring with them their old nature of flesh and blood (1 Cor. 15:50: ". . . flesh and blood cannot inherit the kingdom of God"): "and how can one who is already worn out by the corrupt world understand incorruption?" (4 Ezra 4:11).[55] Indeed, Jesus himself stated positively (Matt. 5:9; Mark 12:25) that they will then be like the angels in heaven, exalted above all earthly needs (cf. *Enoch* 15:3–7), much in the same way as the passage cited in *Enoch*[56] demonstrates the Palestinian view: they will be "spiritual," πνευματικοί. Such a situation, however, presupposes (at least in the case of those who live to see the Parousia) a "transformation," as

55. [Translation from the RSV. Weiss's text reads: *quomodo, qui existis in corrupto saeculo, (poteris) intelligere incorruptionem.* Cf. Charles: "How, then, should it be possible for a mortal in a corruptible world to understand the ways of the Incorruptible?" Robert Henry Charles, *The Apocrypha and Pseudepigrapha of the Old Testament* (Oxford: Clarendon, 1913), 2: 565. With respect to 1 Cor. 15:50 ff., see Joachim Jeremias, "Flesh and Blood Cannot Inherit the Kingdom," *NTS* 2 (1955–56): 151–59, reprinted in Jeremias' book, *Abba* (Göttingen: Vandenhoeck & Ruprecht, 1966), pp. 298–307. Jeremias' interpretation of 1 Cor. 15 is much the same as Weiss's: "This, then seems to be the mystery, the new revelation: the change of the living and the dead takes place immediately at the Parousia" (*Abba*, p. 307). See also Jeremias, *Eucharistic Words,* p. 172.]

56. "Why have you (angels) forsaken the high holy everlasting heaven? . . . while you were yet *spiritual, holy,* and partaking of *eternal life,* you defiled yourselves with women. . . . But before, you were spiritual, enjoying eternal and undying life, for all generations of the world. Therefore I made no women for you."

Paul says (1 Cor. 15:52). They must in some way participate in the παλιγγενεσία [Matt. 19:28].

Indeed, the question arises whether one would not do
better to interpret this term as referring to the transformation of individuals (as -γενεσία seems to suggest), rather
than the world. In Titus 3:5, it is used in connection with
baptism. Is there any other saying of Jesus bearing on this
point? We cannot apply his saying in the discussion with
the Sadducees (Mark 12:25) here, because it has to do
only with those who come into the Kingdom of God
through death and resurrection. They no longer need a
transformation, since they have already laid aside the σάρξ
in death, and have become πνεύματα. Did Jesus express
himself concerning the mystery of the transformation described by Paul in 1 Cor. 15:51 f.? Possibly one can appeal
here to John 3:3, 6, or to the saying underlying it. It seems
to me that there is evidence[57] that a saying of the Lord was
in circulation in the second century, which is also echoed
in 1 Pet. 1:3, 23, and—departing from the Johannine text
(ἄνωθεν)—read approximately as follows: ἐὰν μὴ ἀνα-
γεννηθῆτε, οὐ μὴ εἰσέλθητε εἰς τὴν βασιλείαν τῶν οὐρανῶν.[58] Whether this saying comes from the Logia is not
certain.[59] But one can hardly dispute its basic authenticity.
The suspicion that is raised against it is really based upon
the fact that the saying is explained in terms of Paul or the
Pauline "John," instead of on its own terms. To be sure,
John clearly identifies the ἄνωθεν γέννησις in verse 6 with
what the Christian experiences in baptism, i.e., with what

---

57. Cf. Wilhelm Bousset, *Die Evangeliencitate Justins des Märtyrers in
ihrem Wert für die Evangelienkritik* (Göttingen: Vandenhoeck & Ruprecht, 1891), pp. 151 ff. [Cf. Matt. 18:3; *Thomas* 46b.]
58. "Unless you are born again, you will not enter the Kingdom of
Heaven." (Cf. Justin, *Apology* 1. 61. 7; Ps.-Clement, *Homily* 11. 26;
Clement of Alexandria, *Exhortation to the Greeks* 9. 82.)
59. The expression βασιλεία τῶν οὐρανῶν makes me think it unlikely.

Paul calls καινὴ κτίσις in 2 Cor. 5:17.[60] By this he means
the completely new beginning of an ethical-religious life,
which is there the moment the Spirit of God enters as a new
factor into the life of the individual Christian and begins to
transform it. Is this the same meaning Jesus had in mind?
It seems unlikely, for the fundamental transformation of
life which he demanded of his disciples was consistently
represented as one's own act without any mention of the
Holy Spirit. Must one assume, then, that this deeply religious term, which means an actual transformation by God,
had been used by Jesus merely as a figure of speech: to be
transformed as radically as one who is begotten a second
time? This would be an unwarranted spiritualization of
his real meaning. Let me now raise the question whether
the ἀναγεννᾶσθαι spoken of by Jesus does not refer instead to the transformation of the individual at the Parousia. Everyone who wishes to enter the Kingdom of God
and see its blessings, must experience a new procreation,
a second birth: made from a being of flesh and blood, he
must be made into a πνεῦμα.

10. [THE JUDGMENT AND THE FATE OF THE CONDEMNED]

Another major event, next to the transformation of the
world, is *the Judgment*.[61] It is not certain whether this *follows* the destruction of the old world or *precedes* it. In any
case, it must be examined before we ask about the positive
side of salvation in the Kingdom of God. There can be no

---

60. Cf. Hermann Gunkel, *Die Wirkungen des heiligen Geistes nach der
populären Anschauung der apostolischen Zeit und nach der Lehre des
Apostels Paulus* (Göttingen: Vandenhoeck & Ruprecht, 1888). [See
above, pp. 92 ff.]
61. [Cf. *Predigt²*, pp. 111–113.]

doubt that Jesus regarded this Judgment as *prior* to the establishment of the Kingdom. He was in complete agreement with the Baptist on this point.

There will be many who will attack this thesis, urging that in Jesus' preaching the Judgment is thought of as the conclusion to the "present Kingdom of God," occurring at the συντέλεια τοῦ αἰῶνος (τούτου), as a beginning and preparation for the "Kingdom of completion." One sees that here too the attempt to distinguish two stages in the advent of the Kingdom of God results in hopeless complication. The representatives of this approach[62] support it by reference to such thoroughly secondary passages as Mark 9:1 and Matt. 13:37, 43, 47–50, which can prove nothing. The Matthean passages are written from the viewpoint of the later generation which distinguished the present βασιλεία τοῦ Χριστοῦ from the future Kingdom of God. This conception of the συντέλεια τοῦ αἰῶνος is exactly parallel to the Johannine conception of the ἐσχάτη ἡμέρα. They both speak of this end of things as a definite but still distant time. For them the only things that really matter are the ideas of the present βασιλεία, the immanent ζωή, and the κρίσις of the present time. This reworking of Jesus' idea is of the greatest historical importance—for the first time it made possible a Christian world-history—but it is nevertheless a transformation of the original idea.

If we turn to the accredited sayings of Jesus, Mark 9:43 ff. especially instructs us most clearly as to the relationship between Judgment and the establishment of the Kingdom. Here it is presupposed that those to whom the words

---

62. Even Ernst Issel, *Die Lehre vom Reiche Gottes im Neuen Testament* (Leiden: E. J. Brill, 1891), p. 119, belongs with these. Schmoller, however, opposes this distinction in a first-rate manner. Mark 9:1 can prove nothing, since the decisive words ἐν δυνάμει are not to be found in the parallels, and in any case are a later Paulinizing addition (cf. Rom. 1:4).

are addressed will *live to see* the coming of the Kingdom. And now the alternative is put to them: either to enter into life (v. 45: εἰς τὴν βασιλείαν τοῦ θεοῦ) with a mutilated member or to be thrown into the γέεννα in full possession of all their members. It is evident, therefore, that the way to life or to the βασιλεία leads through the Judgment, in which the fate of the individual is to be decided. Not only will those who are still alive participate in this Judgment, but also the (resurrected) dead; even the other nations, the ancient inhabitants of Sodom and Gomorrah, the "people of Nineveh from the time of Jonah, the Queen of Sheba from the days of Solomon (Matt. 12:41 f.; Luke 11:31 f.)."[63] In Matt. 25:31 f., all the nations even pass before the judgment throne of the Son of man. Very little can be said with precision concerning the fate of the condemned, since Jesus' sayings on this point are not uniform. This much alone is clear: the most grievous part of their punishment is exclusion from the Kingdom of God. This is expressed in the imagery of the parables: some will be thrust out into outer darkness, where there will be wailing and chattering[64] of teeth. This is the dark and dreadful back side of the bright and cheerful picture of salvation in the Kingdom of God described in the same saying: the elect in the bright warm banquet hall at the messianic table with the patriarchs (Matt. 8:11 f.). The formula which is more frequently utilized is derived from this image. One may not, therefore, regard it as an objective description of the

63. Willibald Beyschlag, *Neutestamentliche Theologie; oder, Geschichtliche Darstellung der Lehren Jesu und des Urchristenthums nach den neutestamentlichen Quellen* (Halle: Strien, 1891–1892), 1:200. [Trans. N. Buchanan, *New Testament Theology, or, Historical Account of the Teaching of Jesus and of Primitive Christianity According to the New Testament Sources* (Edinburgh: T. & T. Clark, 1895), 1:204 f.]

64. [In *Predigt²* Weiss noted that he no longer considered this interpretation correct. Instead, he proposed, "βρυγμός does not mean chattering with cold, but gnashing in rage and despair" (p. 112, n. 1.).]

place of the damned, apart from its relationship with that imagery. More often this place is pictured not as one of cold darkness, but as a fiery furnace. Of course this was no metaphor; rather, Jesus, like his contemporaries, evidently was thinking of the gruesome valley near Jerusalem [Gehenna] in which the Israelites once sacrificed their children to Moloch, and where, according to the usual Jewish expectation (cf. *Enoch* 90–91), the great Judgment was to take place. The sayings are ambiguous in regard to the question whether the condemned were ultimately to be burned up completely, i.e., *annihilated,* or subjected to an eternal *torment.* The former is assumed in Mark 8:35; the latter in Matt. 25:41, 46 (eternal fire, eternal punishment), Mark 9:48, and Luke 16:23 ff. To which prospect Jesus inclined cannot be said with certainty.[65]

65. It is more probable that Jesus, following the ancient Israelite view, had in mind a final extermination and annihilation of the persistently disobedient. The verses in Matt. 25:41, 46, were quite possibly first formulated by the redactor of that Gospel; Mark 9:48 has no parallels, and is thus probably an addition by the revisor [cf. Isaiah 66:24]; Luke 16:23 ff. presents a special case. The parable of the rich man and poor Lazarus is derived from the Jewish-Christian (Ebionite) special source of Luke (cf. Paul Feine, *Eine vorkanonische Ueberlieferung des Lukas in Evangelium und Apostelgeschichte* [Gotha: F. A. Perthes, 1891]). This writing, which originated in the later Jerusalem community, seems in general to represent the view that the righteous do not have to wait for the messianic Judgment, but pass over directly after death into the final state of messianic bliss (cf. Luke 23:43, which is also from this source). Likewise in Luke 16:23 ff., "Hades" is not a place merely of a shadowy, but rather of a tormented existence, in contrast to the bosom of Abraham, i.e., Paradise (Luke 23:43; cf. Matt. 8:11 ff.), the messianic realm of joy. Perhaps this source already has the idea (Luke 23:42, according to the following reading: ἐν τῇ βασιλείᾳ σου) that since Christ's ascension, the messianic Kingdom is already established in heaven, under the κύριος τῆς δόξης (James 2:1 f.). This would then be still another development of the idea of the Kingdom of God. [See below, p. 136, n. 100. For a good review and critique of recent interpretations of Jesus' ideas concerning the fate of the condemned, see Alan M. Fairhurst, "The Problem Posed by the Severe Sayings Attributed to Jesus in the Synoptic Gospels," *SJT* 23 (1970): 77–91. Fairhurst's own position is much like Weiss's.]

Absolute clarity as to the kind of punishment to be meted out cannot, therefore, be hoped for. Nevertheless, it is possible to recognize in Jesus' view a distinction of degrees or types of sin, which, however strange it may seem to us, is perfectly natural in Jewish thought. Jesus even recognized a distinction between forgivable and unforgivable sins [Matt. 12:22–32]. Anyone who has ever seriously considered the characteristic severity and forcefulness of Jesus' thought will be astounded not that he actually declared a certain degree of sin to be unforgivable, but rather, that he extended the limits of what constitute forgivable sins as much as he did. What is unforgivable, both in this world and the next, is blasphemy against the Holy Spirit, i.e., the conscious denial that the Holy Spirit is active in the work of Jesus. They lie who accuse Jesus of alliance with the devil or of being possessed. They cannot dispute the superhuman power of Jesus' activities, so they impugn it, and thereby affront God himself. But these are only the leaders of the people. The great mass of the people have not ventured this insolence. To be sure, they have reviled the Son of man—he is a glutton and a wine-boozer, the companion of tax collectors and sinners—but these words are aimed only against his person, not against God himself. It is not yet, therefore, a matter of conscious rebellion, but only of foolish blindness, which the messianic judge commissioned by God will count as sins done in ignorance or as misdemeanors—if the people will repent for them at least at the time of Jesus' resurrection. Sins done in error can be forgiven, for through the sacrifice of his life Jesus made the necessary sin offering for the people, and thereby ransomed them from the otherwise inevitable death penalty. But if at that time there is still no repentance, the offering will be forfeited, and the people abandoned to destruction.

Considered in this light, the sayings of Jesus concerning sentencing to destruction seem more understandable and milder than when we add in modern or Pauline concepts of sin and retribution.

11. THE MEANING OF SALVATION IN THE KINGDOM OF GOD

We now ask: If Jesus proclaimed the Kingdom of God without generally defining this conception more closely for his hearers, what did he understand the impending but still future Kingdom of God to mean? And what did he wish his hearers to understand by it? It is generally conceded that Jesus adopted this concept primarily and predominantly in the sense in which it was understood by his contemporaries and without correcting it. Certainly this is true. But what was this sense? Wellhausen[66] expressed the prevailing viewpoint when he said that the *Malkuth* is always to to be conceived antithetically: the Kingdom *of God* in opposition to another $\beta\alpha\sigma\iota\lambda\epsilon\acute{\iota}\alpha$. But this tells us little, so long as we do not know what, for Jesus, it was opposed to. It has already been shown that in an important passage, Matt. 12:28, the $\beta\alpha\sigma\iota\lambda\epsilon\acute{\iota}\alpha$ $\tau o\hat{\upsilon}$ $\theta\epsilon o\hat{\upsilon}$ is set over against that of Satan. The question arises whether this is only a passing thought or whether it is fundamental to Jesus' way of thinking. Few passages yield any direct evidence. But if in Matt. 12:45 Jesus is describing his experience with this generation, and in this connection uses the idea of demon exorcism; if we note how the demons regard him as the one who has come to destroy them; and if originally all the afflictions which Jesus healed were traced, ultimately, to the

66. Julius Wellhausen, *Die Pharisäer und Sadducäer. Eine Untersuchung zur inneren jüdischen Geschichte* (Greifswald: L. Bamberg, 1874), pp. 23 ff.

influence of Satan (Matt. 8:16–17; Luke 13:16); then we realize that Jesus conceived of his work as a struggle against Satan,[67] and the opposition between God and mammon as really between God and Satan, i.e., between the Kingdom of God and Satan.[68] This opposition also determines the meaning of the salvation brought by the Kingdom of God. As we have seen already, if the Rule of God primarily brings release from all affliction of body and soul (from all *tristitia: Assumption of Moses,* 10:2), then the evil spirits to whom the people have been subjected must give way, for they have lost their power (Luke 10:18).

The deliverance of the people from their enemies and oppressors belongs in this context. There are no direct sayings of Jesus in which the Roman rule is represented as Satan's work,[69] except perhaps Luke 4:6. Yet there can be no doubt that in the $\beta a \sigma \iota \lambda \epsilon i a \ \tau o \hat{v} \ \theta \epsilon o \hat{v}$ this was to be a matter of foremost importance. Some may think that the earthly-political character of the idea must be denied in view of the story about tribute money [Mark 12:17]. But what was expressed here in principle, was shown in practice in John 6:15, and finally emerges clearly in the reprimand of Matt. 11:11 f., is nothing more than the self-evident consequence of what has previously been stated. How can one expect even the slightest inclination on Jesus' part towards any kind of revolutionary act? By force and insurrection men might establish a Davidic monarchy, perhaps even as glorious a kingdom as David's had been; but God will establish the Kingdom of God without human hands, horse, or rider, with only his angels and celestial powers. To hope for the Kingdom of God in the transcendental

---

67. Cf. John 8:32, 43 f.; 12:31; 1 John 3:8.
68. Issel, *Lehre vom Reiche Gottes,* pp. 41 ff., thinks similarly on this point.
69. Luke 22:25 expresses only great disdain.

sense that Jesus understood it and to undertake revolution are as different as fire and water.

Josephus noted as a characteristic of Pharisaic piety that they would rather let themselves be killed than join with the cunning power-politics of the Sadducees. A person of Jesus' markedly religious temperament would necessarily have agreed with them completely. This is not to say that he did not believe in any kind of political restoration; but that only God should bring it about. But when he promises the πραεῖς (Matt. 5:5) that they were to inherit the land of promise, as before him the Psalmist (37:11) and *Enoch* (5:7) had promised they would, this meant that there at last they were to be masters, where now they are still servants. He promises those who yearn for righteousness a complete deliverance from their oppressors and the full restoration of their rights. And, finally, the formula "to possess the Kingdom of God," or "to enter the Kingdom of God" means nothing but this: In this Kingdom, the land of promise, risen anew in more beautiful splendor, will be possessed and ruled by them.[70] This is how the Jewish-Christian psalms in the first two chapters of Luke understand it, especially that of Zechariah, in Luke 1:68 f., 71–75.

By way of counter-evidence, someone might point to the sayings regarding the worthlessness of earthly goods, the danger of riches to the soul, and so forth. But these are only

70. [In *Predigt*[2] Weiss also cites *Enoch* 90:20. He points out that the expressions "entering the Kingdom" and "inheriting the Kingdom" are derived from the ancient idea of "entering" or "inheriting" the Promised Land, namely Israel, "arisen in new glory and splendor" (Ps. 37:11; cf. *Enoch* 5:17). He cites Daniel 7 as basis for the expectation that the righteous would share the task of "ruling" with the Messiah in the Kingdom (Luke 22: 29 f.). This idea obviously had political implications (though Jesus did not stress them), for if the Messiah and the elect were to rule Palestine, "What place is left for the Roman Empire?" (*Predigt*[2], pp. 121 ff.).]

intended as warnings for the time of preparation, admonitions to detach one's self completely from αἰὼν οὗτος in order to be the more fully prepared for the αἰὼν μέλλων. This devaluation of the goods of this αἰών, therefore, proves nothing about the so-called earthly or outward splendor of the future age, because all these valuable things will be present there in a completely different, pure, unworldly, and spiritual condition. They will still be there in the new world, but all that clings to things of flesh and blood, and sin and impurity, will have dropped away. And then, certainly, the θησαυροί (Matt. 6:19 f.) will be opened, the joys of the great messianic banquet, exaltation and power, sitting on the throne and judging—even this is meant concretely and literally—all these things will be refined and transfigured by the heavenly δόξα of God, in whose light all things will shine in splendor. But these "external-political goods"—which are usually mentioned with a shrug of the shoulders and without understanding—are by no means absent from Jesus' picture of the future. And who would really wish to venture that these are only fantasies which have nothing to do with serious thought? To do so, in other words, would be to fail to recognize one of the important characteristics in the portrait of our Lord which makes him tower over prophets, apocalyptists and his contemporaries, namely, that in these things which concern the "color" of the messianic salvation, Jesus was so sparing and, as it were, so conventional. His greatness consisted in the fact that he followed the traditional scheme, but with modesty, reserve and sobriety. He did not allow himself or his disciples to revel in these prospects. He kept his eye all the more seriously on that which according to his entire religious and ethical sensibility was most crucial: what was genuinely religious in the Kingdom of God, and ethical preparation for its coming.

He sounded the mellowest tones, edifying for all time, when he promised comfort to those in sorrow and to the pure in heart that they should see God. To those who would serve peace here, it is promised that there, as sons of God, they may glorify God in the company of the angels.

12. [THE ETHICS OF PREPARATION]

How pure and separate from the things of αἰὼν οὗτος Jesus considered this communion with God to be, appears first of all, however, in the other side of Jesus' preaching.[71] It is a serious and powerful summons to repentance, a summons to turn away from "worldliness," in a word, to intensive preparation for the Kingdom of God.

After the previous discussion, it is hardly necessary to say again that the "righteousness of the Kingdom of God" does not signify the ethical perfection which members of the Kingdom possess or achieve *in the Kingdom of God,* but rather the δικαιοσύνη which is the *condition for entrance into* the Kingdom of God (Matt. 5:20). It is the result of μετάνοια. In accordance with the whole basic religious stance of Jesus, this repentance is understood equally if not more as a negative and ascetic ideal than as a really positive moral one. The new righteousness which Jesus demands of his disciples, who wait with him for the Kingdom of God and hope to enter it, can be understood in neither its negative nor its positive aspects if it is detached from its religious, i.e., in this case, its eschatological context:[72] "Repent, *because* the Kingdom of God has drawn

71. [Cf. *Predigt²*, pp. 138–140.]
72. Therefore the rationalism which conceived of Jesus only as teacher of a new ethics acted just as unhistorically as those who hold the orthodox revelation-faith which regarded the ethical prescriptions of Jesus as generally valid revelations, without taking into account the eschatological apparatus which serves to explain them.

near." The nearness of the Kingdom is the *motive* for the new morality (cf. Luke 12:57—13:9). Can one really construe this "righteousness" of Matt. 5:20 as "morality" in the modern sense of the word? It is, in any case, so thoroughly colored by the religious that we would do better to speak of a new piety, which is just as much a new relationship to God as it is to the world. Its motto is: Seek the Kingdom of God (Luke 12:31), indeed, as Matt. 6:33 properly explains, "first," before all else. Just as in the Lord's Prayer the petition for the coming of the Kingdom of God stands at the beginning, here also, passionate desire for the Kingdom is to be the mood that governs all else. The Kingdom of God is the highest good,[73] as the parables of the pearl and the treasure in the field show, but it is a still distant one, which can be reached only if one gives up everything else for it. This is the meaning of Jesus' demand for repentance, which must be taken quite seriously. For, note carefully, the demand is valid for *all* who hear it, not merely for tax collectors and sinners. The latter's task is relatively easy: they have only to make the fundamental break; they have to turn about ($\dot{\epsilon}\pi\iota\sigma\tau\rho\dot{\epsilon}\phi\epsilon\iota\nu$) to the way of righteousness (Matt. 21:32). Basically, much more is required of the great mass of ordinary people. All have need of repentance, as Luke 13:1–5 says. But for them, repentance involves something else. They are to become like children (Matt. 18:2). Matthew explains this (Matt. 18:4) in terms of the requirement of humility and lowliness.

But is this really the characteristic of children that Jesus had in mind when he set them up as a model? Is it not rather their lack of self-consciousness and directness, and especially their simplicity and unfailing accuracy of perception, gifts which are natural in children but can be granted to

73. [Weiss, himself, questions the appropriateness of this kind of modernizing formula: infra, pp. 133–135.]

adults only by God, which is the altogether wonderful thing? But the same Matthew has arranged several groups of sayings in the Sermon on the Mount in an extremely perceptive order which certainly corresponds to Jesus' meaning. These are the sayings about laying up treasures, about serving two masters and about anxiety, which Matthew grouped around the sayings about the eye [6:19–34]. This evidently was to mean that just as man needs a true, single, and unclouded eye in order to see, so likewise he needs ἁπλότης, simplicity, singlemindedness, if he truly wishes to prepare himself for the Kingdom of God. Whoever waits for the Kingdom dares not be divided, a man with two souls (James 1:6–8). "No one can serve two masters. You cannot serve God and mammon." This saying reflects the thorough opposition between αἰὼν οὗτος and αἰὼν μέλλων, evident throughout Jesus' outlook. For mammon, the demon which reduces man to slavery, is still only one of the agents of the θεὸς τοῦ αἰῶνος τούτου, and therefore stands in exclusive opposition to God. One can serve God and through such service show himself worthy of the coming age (Luke 20:35) only if he tears himself free from that slavery. Therefore one must not gather up treasures on earth, for "where your treasure is, there is your heart," and this heart should not linger on earth with its thoughts and desires,[74] but rather, as Paul said, Christians, though still on earth, already feel themselves to be citizens of heaven (Phil. 3:20), from whence they await the Kingdom of God. That mammon is named in the passage is directly related to the fact that as Jesus saw it wealth is the strongest tie that chains men to this world. It is even so strong that, ordinarily a rich man can be saved for the Kingdom of God only through a divine miracle (Mark 10:27).

To many epochs of Christianity these sayings have

74. Col. 3:2: τὰ ἄνω φρονεῖτε μὴ τὰ ἐπὶ τῆς γῆς.

seemed too hard, and despite the explicit and earnest warning of Jesus that it is easier for a camel to go through the eye of a needle than for a rich man to enter the Kingdom of God, and although Jesus declared, "with men it is *impossible*," many rich Christians, indeed many rich churches have dared to remain rich. I do not believe that it is because they have consciously counted on the saying "with God it is possible," i.e., on a special intervention, for in that case it still would have been much more devout to become poor than to count on a miracle. Instead, I believe that Christianity has, more or less without comment, laid this view of Jesus aside and has sought to compromise the seriousness of the saying by means of all kinds of devious interpretations and erosions of its meaning. It would be more truthful to take one's stand historically with respect to these matters, and to understand them from the perspective of Jesus' eschatological and dualistic viewpoint. Since the rod has been broken over αἰὼν οὗτος, since τὸ σχῆμα τοῦ κόσμου τούτου παράγει (1 Cor. 7:31), money can only be harmful to the soul. It is only a fetter which binds men to a world ruled and corrupted by the devil, whereas they ought to be free of it, in order to await the new world. That money might be a means to moral ends, the foundation of a moral life's work, the tool of good and beneficial activity in the service of God's mankind, does not even come into consideration here. For the world has grown old, and human labor can no longer create anything really good or enduring upon it. God himself must come and make everything new. At most, money is still good for alms for the alleviation of the worst distress.

The same is true with respect to the evaluation of the "ethical goods" and institutions: secular vocation,[75] marriage, and the state. Here it is considerably more difficult

75. [Weiss's term is *bürgerliche Beruf*.]

108

for us to keep the historical facts clearly in view. For if we really do so, it will turn out that our previous understanding of Jesus' sayings, together with the system of Christian ethics which we have developed out of them, has been based upon our indulging in certain qualifications, reinterpretations, and above all, upon our looking at matters from a fundamentally different point of view. The nearest contact Protestant ethics has with the sayings of Jesus is in the area of secular vocation. For at least in the parable of the talents, and indirectly even in the parable of the unjust steward, fidelity in one's calling is declared to be the ideal demanded by God. And even if there were no direct sayings concerning life in one's secular vocation, we would have in Jesus' own sense of calling and conduct of his own life an example which would clearly illumine the religious nature of the performance of one's calling. From this we could draw thousandfold application to the problems of secular vocation.

The fact remains, however, and ought at least to be mentioned, that as concerns our attitude, we perceive the matter of secular vocation today exactly opposite to the way Jesus did. It cannot be denied that from Jesus' standpoint, life in one's secular calling, entanglement in trade and traffic, involved at least *dangers* which should make one glad to give it up for the sake of the Kingdom of God. It is true that we have little in the way of direct sayings to prove this, but the fact that Jesus and his disciples pursued no vocation is sufficient evidence to show that he regarded it as a hindrance to real preparation for the Kingdom of God.

This is even clearer with respect to his opinions on family life. The same Jesus who thought so highly of marriage that he regarded anyone who put marriage asunder as breaking the first marriage [Matt. 19:4 ff.], nevertheless uttered this unprecedentedly sharp saying: "If anyone comes to me

109

and does not *hate* his father and his mother (and his wife)[76]
and his brothers and sisters, yea, even his own life, he cannot be my disciple" (Luke 14:26).

Commenting on this point Wendt says:

> We must first determine whether even in the sayings from
> the Logia, in Luke 14:26, 27–33, where he declares *without
> qualification* that separation from dearest relatives, accept-
> ance of extreme suffering, and renunciation of all possessions
> *whatsoever* were necessary for *all his* disciples, Jesus still had
> in mind the same stipulation which was strictly specified in
> the above-mentioned demands for cutting off hand, foot and
> eye (Mark 9:43 ff.); namely, that the blessings in question
> give an occasion for sin, and could be retained only to the
> detriment of the tasks necessary within the Kingdom of God.
> Now it is not the case, according to Jesus' outlook as ex-
> pressed in other passages, that fellowship with one's earthly
> family, earthly goods, and the earthly life as such are incom-
> patible with the righteousness demanded in the Kingdom of
> God, and must therefore be sacrificed under all circum-
> stances. The same Jesus . . . who spoke the words found in
> Mark 7:10 ff.; 10:1–12; Matt. 5:13 f. . . . cannot at the same
> time have meant and taught that the abandonment of all ties
> to the nearest members of one's family has value as such and
> is commanded for the sake of the Kingdom of God.[77]

These words are quoted *in extenso* because they are typical
of the current interpretation of these things. Even though
these interpreters concede that this demand was addressed
to all disciples generally and without qualification, never-

76. This is probably added by Luke; cf. 18:29.
77. Wendt, *Lehre Jesu,* 2: 382 f. [=*The Teaching of Jesus,* 2: 62 f. The
rendering here is by the present translators. For a recent discussion of
Luke 14:26, see R. A. Harrisville, "Jesus and The Family," *Interpretation*
23 (1969): 429 ff. Harrisville treats such sayings as instances of Jesus'
opposition to Jewish legalism. He does not mention "interim ethics" or
attempt to relate the sayings to Jesus' belief in the imminence of the
Kingdom!]

theless, in their exegesis they add the restrictive clause, "lest these things lead to sin," words never spoken by Jesus. The truth is, however, that Jesus supposed, and in fact said to their faces to those accompanying him, therefore probably even to the great crowds which were favorable to him (Luke 14:25 f.), that this requirement applied to *all of them*. All of them will find their family life and their usual human relationships brought to ruin. All, therefore, come under the requirement. Surely it cannot be that these most ethical relationships which were ordained by God could ever come to grief, even under extraordinary circumstances! But Jesus assumes that this is the rule![78] This would be shocking and inconceivable had Jesus meant here to proclaim an ethical law for his church, a requirement for "the members of the Kingdom of God." No—this cannot have been what Jesus meant, for in the Kingdom of God there is no marriage at all. Jesus was impressed by the zeal of this ὄχλοι, but struck with deep sadness on account of their well-meant but basically superficial way of life, and saw in them only a crowd of plan-makers and sanguine optimists, who still lacked the slightest suspicion as to what really was required of them (Luke 14:28–33). He knows —however much goodwill they may have, however much they may even long for the Kingdom of God with all their might—that so long as they continue in their former relationships, they will not be able to succeed in the ζητεῖν τὴν βασιλείαν which he demands. He summons them, therefore, to the frightful challenge, like the physician who confronts his patient with the choice between a perilous operation or letting things take their course. A half-remedy will not do. A half-preparation, a limping between two sides, a

---

78. That μισεῖν does not mean the intention of hurting one's family, but only complete inner detachment from them (Wendt, *Lehre Jesu*, 2: 382 f.) is obvious.

serving of two masters, is impossible. How can one under-stand these heroic words, by which ever so many bonds of tender affection are to be torn asunder, from any other standpoint than this: the things of this world, however high and godly they may be in themselves, have lost all value now that the world is ripe for destruction? Now they can only hinder and hold back. Cast them away, and grasp at what comes from above with both hands. Wendt recalls Luther's verse:

Though they take our body, goods, rank, child and wife,
Let them go, they matter not.

To construe these words as merely figurative is to weaken and falsify their meaning. "We must understand these words as arising from the mood of battle, when such ex-treme external sacrifices for the sake of the Gospel—which in the periods of peace after the victory appear only as pos-sibility and exception—must be regarded as a matter of necessity and principle." I might well point out that Luther's words originate not only in a mood of battle, but in a completely eschatological mood, or at least one of prep-aration for death. "The Kingdom must remain ours!" "Though they take our body. . . ." All this makes it clear that it is not meant as a regulation governing the behavior of a permanent moral community. Instead, it is the watch-word for the few who know that everything now rests on the edge of the sword: at any moment death or (in Jesus' sense) the destruction of the world can break in upon us. And, therefore, let us be free from everything that pulls us down and would hold us here!

A further comment about Jesus' attitude toward the state might almost be superfluous. One should not read more into the saying about tribute money than was meant by it. Jesus intends no more than to repudiate revolution;

not, however, because the state is ordained by God as the sphere of an ethical activity, but rather, because it is *impious* to anticipate God's action. He gives his Kingdom; it does not come by the hand of man.[79]

We see from this historical survey that our modern Protestant ethic, which certainly is not a human creation but is disclosed through "men of God,"[80] does not represent a simple application of the teaching of Jesus. Jesus' prophetic demands were born out of a religious attitude which, at any rate, in this form we cannot expect to relive in our daily experience, but only, at most, once each century. And it is important, therefore, to make clear to ourselves that, just as we always sing Luther's words with a few reservations and modifications, so likewise, we cannot mean Jesus' words in the exact sense that was originally in-

79. This view of "righteousness" (not *"of* the Kingdom of God," but *"for* the Kingdom of God") could, of course, only remain a sketch in the present writing. [Weiss noted later (*Predigt²,* pp. 134 f.) that the 1892 edition of his work had provoked the charge that it had tied Jesus' ethical preaching too closely to his eschatological proclamation, that it had presented Jesus' world-view too one-sidedly and exaggerated the negative, ascetic and world-renouncing aspects of his ethics. Weiss concedes that this charge is, to a certain extent, fair, but remarks that he had indicated here in the first edition that his account of Jesus' ethics could only be given in the form of a "sketch" and was, necessarily, incomplete. He then describes certain segments of Jesus' ethical message which he believed were not tied up with his eschatological outlook: "those maxims which are full of the purest and deepest wisdom . . . which simply and serenely stated what his pure, clear and godly soul perceives as self-evident" (pp. 135 f.); his antipharisaic ethics; and his endorsement of the "double-love commandment" (pp. 137 f.). Weiss goes on, however, to insist that Jesus did *not* expect history or the world to continue, and that "the new morality which he preaches is thought of as *condition* for entrance into the Kingdom of God" (pp. 138 f.). He develops this latter point in greater detail, pp. 138–154. See also above, pp. 10 f., 52 f.]

80. [See Johannes Weiss, *Die Nachfolge Christi und die Predigt der Gegenwart* (Göttingen: Vandenhoeck & Ruprecht, 1895), pp. 173 f., where he refers to Luther, Goethe and Carlyle, apparently in the·same sense. Cf. above also pp. 16–18.]

tended. If this is clear to us theologians, then perhaps it will not hurt if our congregations come to know something about it too.

Thus we learn from the foregoing discussion that as Jesus conceived of it, the Kingdom of God is a radically superworldly entity which stands in diametric opposition to this world. This is to say that there *can* be no talk of an *innerworldly* development of the Kingdom of God in the mind of Jesus! On the basis of this finding, it seems to follow that the dogmatic religious-ethical application of this idea in more recent theology,[81] an application which has completely stripped away the original eschatological-apocalyptical meaning of the idea, is unjustified. Indeed, one proceeds in an only apparently biblical manner if one uses the term in a sense different from that of Jesus. For more on this point, see our concluding remarks [Infra, pp. 131 ff.].

13. [JESUS' FUTURE ROLE: THE SON OF MAN]

But for some time the reader will have been asking impatiently, what then, if such is the case, is the difference between Jesus and the Baptist? They both preach only the nearness of the Kingdom of God; they call men to repentance and gather a circle of disciples who prepare themselves for the coming of the Kingdom. What is unique about the activity and the person of Jesus that distinguishes him from all the apocalyptic preachers? Here "activity" and "person" must be clearly differentiated! For, as we have already seen above, the activity of Jesus is certainly, in principle, no different from that of John. Both men are moved by the overwhelming certainty that God is about to assert his rule.

81. [I.e., Ritschlian.]

They both employ every means to make the people ready for their encounter with God. And in the same way that John would have thought it a pretentious sacrilege to believe that he himself could bring the Kingdom of God to pass, so for Jesus too, such a "founding" or "establishing" of the Kingdom on the part of men would have been unthinkable. For him also the thing to do was to wait and to work in preparation for the Kingdom.[82]

One basic difference is that in John's own opinion (Luke 3:16), as well as in Jesus' (Luke 7:28), John would have a place in the Kingdom of God like that of others. Jesus, on the other hand, was aware that in this Kingdom he himself would be the "Messiah," the King. Here we come to the final and most important point, which is at the same time the principal problem with which any theology must come to terms, namely, that of Jesus' *messianic self-consciousness*.[83] The experience at his baptism is the birthplace of this consciousness. Whatever form the event may have taken, it is certain that here Jesus became convinced that he was *the* Son of God whom God had appointed to bring in the messianic future. Baldensperger has rendered a service in stressing the fact that this certainty felt by Jesus, though far from being a clear and objective concept, was altogether *religious* in character. Thus it bore all the marks of a certainty of faith: utter firmness of conviction, yet consciousness of an enormous paradox; with all the fervor of the con-

---

82. [See above, pp. 74–81.]

83. The following discussion will show especially how much I am indebted to Baldensperger's book, *Das Selbstbewusstsein Jesu* (see above, n. 26). This indebtedness may be seen in the preceding discussion as well. [Weiss develops his interpretation of Jesus' "messianic self-consciousness" and the "Son of man" at greater length in *Predigt*[2], pp. 154–178. His position is not essentially different, but he does state more forcefully that Jesus did not think of himself as Messiah or Son of man *in the present;* rather he expected that with the manifestation of the Kingdom he would *become* the Messiah or Son of man (pp. 166, 175).]

sciousness of sonship (Matt. 11:27), nevertheless humble shock at the audacity of this idea; absolute clarity as to the course of the future, yet a complete uncertainty as to the means and path that were to lead to it. Indeed, how should the carpenter's son from Nazareth, even after hearing that voice from heaven, ever imagine that he would be the Messiah? At the very most, the idea of the rule of David might have occurred to him. For even if he repudiated the way of revolution, it still would have been possible and conceivable that by some special act God might exalt him as King of his people. But even if he let people call him by the title "Son of David," he nevertheless repudiated it as an inappropriate characterization of the Messiah. As evidence for this, see his conversation with the scribes in Mark 12:30 ff. This can only signify, as Baldensperger rightly remarks, that the Messiah must be more than an heir and successor to the throne of David, however magnificent such a one might be: according to the scripture he must be David's *Lord,* to whom even David looks up with reverence. This means that Jesus turned away from the Davidic conception of the Messiah to a loftier image of the Messiah. For Jesus, the proper form in which the figure of the Messiah was to be thought of was the Son of man of Daniel and *Enoch.*[84]

84. The theory of Paul Anton de Lagarde (*Göttingische Gelehrte Anzeigen,* 1891, pp. 507 ff.) that Daniel 7 dates from A.D. 69 breaks down, to mention only one point, at 7:25, where Antiochus Epiphanes *alone,* and no one else, can be meant. Be that as it may, Lagarde's essay imposes upon theology the duty of examining the book of Daniel with respect to its integrity (which I, too, have questioned for some time). If one were to read Daniel 9 in the *Apocalypse of Baruch* or *Ezra,* it would not occur to him to doubt that the author wrote *after* A.D. 70. Could it be that the book of Daniel, and thus even certain parts of chapter 7, was edited after A.D. 70? [Since Weiss's time, many scholars have urged that *Enoch,* or, at any rate, the Similitudes of Enoch (*En.* 37–69) can have no value as a source for pre-Christian Judaism because of its late date. Matthew Black, however, has defended the Similitudes' usefulness as a clue to pre-Christian Jewish messianism, while proposing that the conception of the

This idea, as Baldensperger properly emphasizes, expresses a purely religious and thoroughly transcendental messianic hope, in which it is not human but only divine intervention that settles matters. The more transcendent Jesus' vision of the Son of man clad in heavenly splendor, the more prominent was the purely religious character of this self-consciousness; but at the same time, his own relationship to that figure became more problematic. Be that as it may, Jesus chose this self-designation as the most suitable expression of his attitude towards the messiahship, and thereby bequeathed to our theology one of the greatest and most difficult problems we have, one which up until today has not found a definitive solution.[85]

Son of man contained here represents a reworking of the earlier idea found in *En.* 70–71 ("The Eschatology of the Similitudes of Enoch," *JTS*, n.s. 3 (1952): 1–10.]
85. [Heinz E. Tödt has furnished a thorough study of this title in his recent monograph, *The Son of Man in the Synoptic Tradition*, trans. D. M. Barton (Philadelphia: Westminster, 1965). Tödt, like Bultmann, believes that when Jesus spoke of the coming of the Son of man, he was expecting someone other than himself to fill that role. It has recently been argued that the "Son of man" Christology is entirely secondary: Ph. Vielhauer, "Jesus und der Menschensohn," *ZThK* 60 (1963): 133–77; Howard M. Teeple, "The Origin of the Son of Man Christology," *JBL* 84 (1964): 213–50. Vielhauer believes that this Christology originated in the primitive Palestinian Church; Teeple traces it to a later Hellenistic-Jewish Christianity. Eduard Schweizer, on the other hand, proposes that Jesus identified himself with the Son of man: he would be "both counsel for the defense and for the prosecution" at the last judgment. But the idea that the Son of man would be judge comes from a later Jewish-Christian segment of the church: Ed. Schweizer, "The Son of Man," *JBL* 79 (1960): 119–29; "The Son of Man Again," *NTS* 9 (1962–63): 256–61. Among the plethora of recent literature on the subject, the following articles might also be mentioned: Peter C. Hodgson, "The Son of Man and the Problem of Historical Knowledge," *JR* 41 (1961): 91–108; Joachim Jeremias, "Die älteste Schicht der Menschensohn-Logien," *ZNW* 58 (1967): 159–72; Robert Maddox, "The Function of the Son of Man According to the Synoptic Gospels," *NTS* 15 (1968): 45–74. Recently it has been suggested that Jesus may have applied the term "Son of man" to himself as a "euphemism" [circumlocution?] for

117

Our attempt at explaining this begins with an apparent superficiality. How does it happen that when Jesus speaks of the Son of man he always speaks in the third person, thus speaking of himself in an objective manner? To be sure, this form also occurs in Matt. 11:27 and Mark 13:32, but here perhaps it is the residue of a certain parabolic manner of speaking. In the majority of cases where the term "Son of man" occurs, it seems to me to imply a kind of abbreviated hint of prophecy. So, for example, in the majority of parousia sayings, one might well supply something like the following: then "the prophecy that the 'Son of man' comes on the clouds of heaven will be fulfilled." And one need put the term "Son of man" mentally in quotation marks only once to realize that reference to prophecy is implied in these predictions of the Parousia. The "Son of man" (namely, Daniel's) will come in his kingly rule (Matt. 16:28). If one understands all this, one will also understand why it was that, when Jesus wished to make clear the certainty of his Second Coming, he did not say "I will come again," but chose instead this familiar, firmly established scriptural term.

Jesus' use of the term is more difficult, however, in those passages in which he is referring to his present appearance, namely, the passion announcements and the saying about the foxes (Matt. 8:19 f.). Here there is but one explanation: the term is not a simple self-designation, but was chosen with special purpose, as if to put quotation marks around it. To the scribe who wanted to follow him, he said

"Son of God": J. Massingberd Ford, " 'The Son of Man'—a Euphemism?", *JBL* 87 (1968): 257–66. See also the monographs by A. J. B. Higgins, *Jesus and the Son of Man* (Philadelphia: Fortress, 1964) and Frederick H. Borsch, *The Son of Man in Myth and History* (Philadelphia: Westminster, 1967). Borsch deals with the ancient myth of the Primal Man. It is safe to say, in 1971, that the Son of man question still "has not found a definitive solution."]

118

in effect: "You believe that you find in me the Messiah, the Son of man. And so you expect to find glory and honor in following me. But be prepared for something different: The 'Son of man,' who is destined for heavenly lordship, is the one who has nowhere to lay his head." The effect of the saying lies in the contrast. This is even more true in the case of the passion announcements. That the "Son of man," whom one can only imagine appearing in glory, must suffer and die, is unheard of. To be sure, this is only a stage through which he must pass, for *after* his death the Son of man will receive everything that people expect to be his in his $\delta \acute{o} \xi \alpha$.[86]

We will now claim provisionally the following result: in the group of parousia sayings, the predicate Son of man means everything will be fulfilled (that is to say, in me) which is prophesied about the Son of man. In the group of passion announcements, the term is borrowed to some degree from the mouth of his adherents, and forms a contrast to the passion announcement. The one of whom you expect the highest things, who seems to you destined to be the "Son of man"—must experience privation, suffer, and die. But in none of these cases is the predicate a plain and simple self-designation. This is not surprising, however. In fact, from the Jewish standpoint, such a usage would have been grotesque. For how can a man, a simple rabbi in Jesus' situation, regard himself as the Son of man? One could not imagine a greater contrast between this name and the reality. Therefore Jesus' employment of the title seems to be meant more as a claim than as an actual self-designation.

Perhaps John 3:14 sheds light on Jesus' meaning. It has long been recognized that the equation of the exaltation with the crucifixion may perhaps be correct from the stand-

86. [Weiss seems to have in mind Mark 10:37–45, 14:62, and possibly 13:26.]

point of the evangelists (John 12:32 f.), but that such cannot have been what Jesus had in mind. For the *tertium comparationis* with which the bronze serpent is compared is not death, but solely the elevation before the eyes of the people. They have to be able to behold the Savior; therefore, he must be raised from his insignificant existence to a glorious height. If we may use this Johannine saying here, we learn what otherwise we would have to infer as hypothesis: that Jesus hoped for an "exaltation," an exaltation through which it must become unmistakably clear to all the people that he was the Son of man. When Jesus used the title, therefore, it is to be understood only in this sense of a claim, the certain hope that this office would be conferred upon him. In any case, he did not call himself this in the same way as he could have called himself, for instance, a son of David or a prophet. He *is* a prophet before the eyes of all. But he is to *become* the Son of man, whether at some point during his lifetime, or, as he became ever more convinced, after he had passed through death.

This interpretation of the messianic title receives noteworthy corroboration from the old Jewish-Christian source which runs through certain parts of the Gospel of Luke and the Book of the Acts and which, in its essentials, originated in Jerusalem circles in the sixties.[87] It did not occur to the early Jewish-Christian community to say that Jesus of Nazareth was the Messiah when he went about on earth battling the devil (Acts 10:38). Again and again this source designates the earthly Jesus as προφήτης,[88] and Peter declares quite clearly that God *made* the Jesus whom the Jews crucified Lord and Messiah through the resurrection and exaltation (Acts 2:36). This is the only way a Jew

---

87. See Paul Feine, *Eine vorkanonische Ueberlieferung* (see above, n. 65), and [Weiss's review of it in] *Theologische Literaturzeitung* [17. Jahrgang, no. 11 (May, 1892), cols. 273–76].

88. Luke 7:16, 39; 13:33; 24:19; Acts 3:22; 7:37, 52.

could think of it, and even Paul advocates this. For the name which is given Jesus at his exaltation, the name which is above every name (Phil. 2:9), is naturally the name "Messiah," and Rom. 1:4 is in complete accord with this interpretation we have offered. Jesus was already υἱὸς τοῦ θεοῦ when he was still alive in the σάρξ, but he first became υἱὸς τοῦ θεοῦ ἐν δυνάμει through the exaltation. Therefore, so long as he was on earth, his messiahship was only a claim, a title to be inherited, which only came into effect when he entered into possession of his κληρονομία which consisted in the heavenly δόξα (Rom. 8:17). On this basis, we are surely justified in taking the view that by using the title "Son of man," Jesus undoubtedly designated himself as the Messiah, not in the sense of a simple self-designation, but rather in the sense of a claim arising out of strong faith. At least this is the meaning in the two principal groups of sayings, the parousia sayings and the passion predictions.

To be sure, these do not exhaust all the evidence. The most difficult passages have not yet been discussed. Matt. 16:13 is often named as the starting point for the whole subject. When Jesus asks here: "Who do the people say that the Son of man is?" and receives this reply: "You are the Messiah," this is ordinarily taken as proof that Son of man and Messiah cannot be the same thing. For Jesus supposes that the title "Son of man" is familiar to the disciples and intelligible to them without need for question or further explanation. The only matter in doubt is whether they will ascribe the title of Messiah to this son of man. But this interpretation betrays the false critical standpoint from which its representatives proceed. A glance at the parallels demonstrates what is evident upon closer scrutiny of the first evangelist, that the editor of Matthew was so familiar with "Son of man" as a designation for the person of Jesus that he simply substituted it for the original μέ found in the parallels. We have here only a further proof[89] that the First Gospel is more secondary in character than the others. This passage, therefore, tells *absolutely nothing* as to the sense in which Jesus spoke of himself as "Son of man." But it does nevertheless teach something of interest. If it is true that "Son of man" was Jesus' customary self-designation and that the early communities found nothing strange about this title since they thought of Jesus as existing in heaven with this name and form (Acts 7:56), and hoped to see him again as such, then it is quite possible and *a priori* probable, that the earliest recorders of Jesus' words (just as in the case of Matt. 16:23) inserted the name "Son of man" in those places where Jesus could have spoken only in the first person. In fact, there are a number of passages in which the name has no significance as a self-designation, but is, as such, absurd and unnatural, e.g., Matt. 11:19 = Luke 7:34. In this Logia passage, where the only concern is to compare the appearance of the prophet Jesus with that of the Baptist, without any kind of eschatological or messianic characteristics, the term υἱὸς τοῦ ἀνθρώπου is extremely strange. What is this title which contains the messianic claim supposed to mean to people who surely would have had to regard its use here as sheer and absurd presumption? How were the people supposed to understand that Jesus spoke here of himself, for they could by no means have granted the supposition that he was the "Son of man"? Even if Jesus had here deliberately laid claim to this rank, the term remains quite irrelevant to the question of Jesus' messiahship. Here it is only equivalent to "I."

---

89. Despite Holsten. [Holsten maintained the priority of an Aramaic Matthew to Mark. C. Holsten, *Die drei ursprünglichen, noch ungeschriebenen Evangelien* (Karlsruhe: Reuther, 1883); *Die synoptischen Evangelien nach der Form ihres Inhaltes* (Heidelberg: K. Groos, 1886).]

It seems to me most natural to assume that it was the transcriber of the tradition who first inserted the familiar title in this passage. What would this term, expressive of the deepest secret of Jesus' faith and hope, have been doing in this unceremonious place?

But two sayings remain which no previous interpretation has been able to make intelligible. These are the two Markan passages 2:10 and 2:28.[90] It is not that they are placed on Jesus' lips so early in Mark's Gospel that makes them strange. The problem is, rather, that in these passages the title "Son of man" is absolutely unintelligible to his opponents. The matter is simple enough, yet usually it is glossed over. Jesus had proclaimed to the paralytic the remission of his sins, and thereby brought upon himself the charge of blasphemy. Who can forgive sins, but God alone? Jesus had said: "So that you know that the Son of man has full authority to forgive sins. . . ."[91] Now none of his opponents doubted that the Messiah has this authority! But they would be quite opposed to any supposition on Jesus' part that *he himself was the Messiah*. This combination of ideas would be altogether absurd! The passage is understandable only in terms of the thesis of Baur, de Lagarde, et al., who see in υἱὸς τ. ἀνθρώπου (בר אנש) no more than a Hebraistic expression for "man." Naturally this is not what it means to Mark, who, as the use of the article ὁ before υἱός shows, finds the messianic title here as in other passages. Very likely, however, Jesus had used the term in the Hebra-

90. [Weiss treats these two passages more closely in an excursus in *Predigt²*, pp. 203–208. He continued to maintain that in both places when Jesus spoke of the Son of man, he meant other men, not merely himself.]

91. [Cf. G. H. Boobyer, "Mark 2:10a and the Interpretation of the Healing of the Paralytic," *HTR* 47 (1954): 115–20. Boobyer believes that the clause was written as an editorial "remark to the Christian *readers* of the Gospel," so that "you" = "Christian readers" (p. 120).]

istic sense, "man." The complaint raised was that Jesus arrogated to himself something that was a matter for God and not for a man. Jesus wished to refute this accusation by demonstrating through the greater, viz., healing, that the lesser, viz., authority to forgive sins, had also been granted to men. Not that it was granted to all times and to every man, but now, at the door to the messianic age, man, or mankind, received this divine prerogative.[92] This interpretation is confirmed by the text of Matthew. B. Weiss has proposed that Matthew is not dependent here on Mark, but presents an original version. This much-contested thesis proves itself here brilliantly. For Matt. 9:8 is in accord with the idea we have suggested, and cannot at all support the usual interpretation: ἰδόντες δὲ οἱ ὄχλοι ἐφοβήθησαν καὶ ἐδόξασαν τὸν θεὸν τὸν δόντα ἐξουσίαν τοιαύτην τοῖς ἀνθρώποις. Thus in the judgment of the people it is also praiseworthy that God has transferred a divine authority to mankind in the person of Jesus.[93]

The situation in Mark 2:28 is the same as in 2:10, in that here too the evidence set before his opponents is null and void so long as they do not admit that Jesus is the Son of man. But at this point another circumstance has to be considered,[94] namely, that the saying in 2:27 is missing in

92. [The "men" who may now forgive sins are not all men or men generally, but the "elect," the saints who will share with Jesus the task of ruling the world. The reference to the forgiveness of sins does not show that Jesus thought himself to be the Messiah; but like the healing of the sick, it showns that the Kingdom is coming, at which time the saints will rule the world (*Predigt²*, p. 207). Cf. Matt 6:12. In preparation for the coming of the Kingdom, Jesus' disciples were both to forgive sins and to pray for forgiveness of their own offenses.]

93. [See, however, on Matt 9:8, Wolfgang Schenk, "Den Menschen," *ZNW* 54 (1963): 272–75. Schenk reads "for," i.e., "for the good of" men rather than "to" men.]

94. My colleague, Lic. Dr. Alfred Rahlfs, on the occasion of his promotion to Licentiate, championed a similar thesis with respect to Mark 2:28, and if I am not in complete agreement with his exposition, nevertheless

the parallels in Matthew and Luke. For this reason it might be thought that the verse should be disregarded as an addition by Deutero-Mark to "A." However, the idea expressed in Mark 2:27 is the only one that makes any reasonable sense here. For all of Jesus' sayings about the Sabbath ultimately mean that the Sabbath exists for the benefit of men, and that man is not to be a slave to the Sabbath. For this saying, Mark intends it *to follow* in verse 28 ($\overset{\scriptscriptstyle\sim}{\omega}\sigma\tau\epsilon$), that the Son of man has the right of free disposal over the Sabbath. Now this conclusion is completely unjustified. What really must follow, rather, is something much more significant, namely, that man generally, not merely the Messiah, can dispose of the Sabbath for his own use.[95] That this is true for the Messiah is obvious. Therefore it appears that in verse 28, $\nu\grave{\iota}\grave{o}\varsigma\ \tau o\hat{\nu}\ \grave{\alpha}\nu\theta\rho\acute{\omega}\pi o\nu$ (not in Mark's sense, but in Jesus') is to be regarded as a designation for "man." It will then follow that verse 27 and verse 28 are not related to each other as premise and inference, but as two *parallels*. Formulated in somewhat different ways, it is declared in both that man is lord over the Sabbath, and may employ it for his own benefit. When the redactor edited the earlier writing, "A," he retained the

I gladly acknowledge that I am obliged to him for hinting that the solution to the difficulty is to be found in the text.

95. [F. W. Beare considers it unthinkable that such could have been Jesus' meaning, and so assigns it to the apostolic church of Palestine, "in controversy with the Pharisees, who took exception to the failure of Christian Jews to keep the Sabbath" ("The Sabbath Was Made for Man?", *JBL* 79 (1960): 135). Why these Jewish Christians would have ceased to observe the Sabbath, Beare does not say. Most modern commentators consider the verse authentic, but refer it to Jesus' own messianic, or, at any rate, eschatological prerogatives. L. S. Hay, however, has recently endorsed the view that "son of man" in Mark 2:10 and 28 means simply "man." But Hay, like Beare, attributes the saying to the early Church: "Both are intended to validate the actions of the members of the Christian community." "The Son of Man in Mark 2:10 and 2:28," *JBL* 89 (1970): 69-75.]

words ὁ υἱὸς τοῦ ἀνθρώπου (with the article) which were already present in the text, and inserted the saying (v. 27) without noticing that he was putting next to one another two originally parallel sayings. The connection which he made between them with the word ὥστε is assuredly awkward.

We may summarize what has been said about the title Son of man as follows: in one group of sayings (Mark 2:10, 28), the title is mistakenly understood by the evangelists as if Jesus had designated himself on these occasions as Messiah, while in fact the expression originally meant only "man"; in a second group, the evangelists have inserted the current name "Son of man" in place of the first person singular, with the result that nothing can be learned from these passages (Matt. 11:19; 16:13) as to the meaning that Jesus ascribed to the title. The third and fourth groups comprise the passion and parousia sayings. In these sayings, Jesus characterizes himself both indirectly and objectively as the one to whom the messianic predicate "Son of man" belongs.

There is still one more passage to be discussed here, one that casts a critical light on the sense in which Jesus used the term: John 5:26 f. Whether this saying was spoken by Jesus or not, it nevertheless expresses precisely the meaning which we believe is signified by the synoptic sayings, only it is much clearer. The Father has given the Son full authority to execute judgment *because he is* υἱὸς ἀνθρώπου. This saying shows clearly that "being Son" meant something other to him than "being Son of man." Jesus is truly Son of God during his earthly ministry; he lives and breathes in the blessed awareness of enjoying his Father's fullest confidence. But he is not yet "Son of man" so long as he has not received the full authority of messianic judgment. On the other hand, he has claim to this full authority, because he is "Son of man." We see, therefore, that even in his lifetime Jesus has this office, but it is the office of the claimant, of the heir. The rule, the inheritance, already belongs to him, but he has not yet taken possession of it.

On this basis we have the answer to the question as to what position Jesus understands himself to have in the Kingdom of God. In the present, he wants to be no more than διδάσκαλος καὶ κύριος of his disciples (John 13:13), but he will be more in the future: the messianic Judge, whom the Baptist promised would be "one who is mightier," the King (Matt. 25:31, 34; Luke 23:42) before whose throne of judgment all peoples, but especially the Jewish people, must appear. Undoubtedly in doing so he is only carrying out God's decisions; for only those for whom it is prepared by God will be given a share in the rule over their fellow members of God's Kingdom (Mark 10:40). Specifically, his twelve disciples, who have endured all testings with him, will be made rulers (an office which consists principally in κρίνειν) over the twelve tribes of Israel (Luke 22:28 ff.). But because it is Jesus who, above all others, humbled himself while on earth, it is he who will receive rule over all the members of the future Kingdom of God.

It may be asked how Jesus thought of his position in relation to God. Did he intend, with Paul (1 Cor. 15:24 f.) and Matt. 13:43, that after his victory over the enemy or after a certain period of ruling, perhaps after a thousand years (Rev. 20:4), the βασιλεία would be given back to God? Or did he mean that this fellowship of the Kingdom, with the Χριστός at its head, would serve God, so that a new heaven would span the new earth, in which God would reign as before, but now over a perfected humanity? Or did he think of his messianic dominion as a joint governorship with the Father (Rev. 3:21; 7:15, 17)? The fact that these different viewpoints are to be found in primitive Christianity constitutes ample evidence that we do not have clear and definite declarations by Jesus on this subject.

From a religious standpoint, the question is relatively unimportant. The important thing is that by virtue of his baptismal experience, Jesus reached the religious conviction that he had been chosen to be Judge and Ruler in the Kingdom of God. This notion has something strange about it for our modern way of thinking, but also for the religious imagination. It is extremely difficult for us to think our way into this self-consciousness.

A few comments may be offered by way of explanation and introduction: Jesus' messianic self-consciousness is only understandable within the framework of his consciousness of sonship. He could understand this commission from God and make it his own only because even prior to this experience, his soul in some way lived in God in a fashion analogous to nothing we can imagine. Only the man who has for a long time ceased to live his own life, but lives rather in and for God, is able to feel himself called to be a prophet without spiritual presumption or falsehood. He alone may and can believe himself to be the Messiah in truth and without fanaticism, to whom it is in some measure natural that he should be entrusted with all things by God because he has opened and offered his soul to God without reservation. One more comment might be added: the sovereignty to which Jesus is called is distinct from all human sovereignties in that it is achieved through service and sacrifice. The heavenly crown which he will wear as "Son of man" is like the crown of thorns, at least to the extent that there can be no question of presumption because of it. Even in all the glory of the heavenly splendor, it will be the highest and most precious task of God's Anointed continually to lead the members of his Kingdom into the presence of

God, in worship and humility before the Father. It will be as the Book of Revelation says: the Lamb . . . will be their shepherd and he will guide them to springs of living water (Rev. 7:17).

To be sure, not all of the questions which surround the "messianic self-consciousness of Jesus" have even been touched upon in the preceding discussion. That was not the problem with which we were primarily concerned here. We meant only to show that the messianic consciousness of Jesus, as expressed in the name Son of man, also participates in the thoroughly transcendental and apocalyptic character of Jesus' idea of the Kingdom of God, and cannot be dissociated from it.

[SUMMARY]

Let me now summarize once more the principal results of our study:

1) Jesus' activity is governed by the strong and unwavering feeling that the messianic time is imminent. Indeed, he even had moments of prophetic vision when he perceived the opposing kingdom of Satan as already overcome and broken. At such moments as these he declared with daring faith that the Kingdom of God had actually already dawned.

2) In general, however, the actualization of the Kingdom of God has yet to take place. In particular, Jesus recognized no preliminary actualization of the rule of God in the form of the new piety of his circle of disciples, as if there were somehow two stages, a preliminary one, and the Kingdom of Completion. In fact, Jesus made no such distinction. The disciples were to pray for the coming of the Kingdom, but men could do nothing to establish it.

3) Not even Jesus can bring, establish, or found the

Kingdom of God; only God can do so. God himself must take control. In the meantime, Jesus can only battle against the devil with the power imparted to him by the divine Spirit, and gather a band of followers who, with a new righteousness, with repentance, humility and renunciation, await the Kingdom of God.

4) The messianic consciousness of Jesus consists of the certainty that when God has established the Kingdom, judgment and rule will be transferred to him. God will raise him to the office of "Son of man" (John 3:14), to which he is entitled (John 5:27), and will *make* him Lord and Messiah (Acts 2:36).

5) Although Jesus initially hoped to live to see the establishment of the Kingdom, he gradually became certain that before this could happen, he must cross death's threshold, and make his contribution to the establishment of the Kingdom in Israel by his death. After that, he will return upon the clouds of heaven at the establishment of the Kingdom, and do so within the lifetime of the generation which had rejected him.

Jesus does not fix the time when this will take place more exactly, since the coming of the Kingdom cannot be determined in advance by observation of signs or calculation.

6) But when it comes, God will destroy this old world which is ruled and spoiled by the devil, and create a new world. Even mankind is to participate in this transformation and become like the angels.

7) At the same time, the Judgment will take place, not only over those who are still alive at the coming of the Son of man, but also over those who will then be raised from the dead, good and evil, Jews and Gentiles alike.

8) The land of Palestine will arise in a new and glorious splendor, forming the center of the new Kingdom. Alien peoples will no longer rule over it, but will come to ac-

knowledge God as Lord. There will be neither sadness nor sin; instead those who are in God's Kingdom shall behold the living God, and serve him in eternal righteousness, innocence, and bliss.

9) Jesus and his faithful ones will rule over this new-born people of the twelve tribes, which will include even the Gentiles.

10) The rule of God is not suspended by the rule of the Messiah, but thereby actualized, whether it be that they reign together side by side, or that Jesus reigns under the higher sovereignty of God.

[CONCLUSIONS]

The results just summarized present peculiar difficulties for systematic and practical theology. Jesus' idea of the Kingdom of God appears to be inextricably involved with a number of eschatological-apocalyptical views which systematic theology has been accustomed to take over without critical examination. But now it is necessary to inquire whether it is really possible for theology to employ the idea of the Kingdom of God in the manner in which it has recently been considered appropriate. The question arises whether it is not thereby divested of its essential traits and, finally, so modified that only the name still remains the same. Thus, for example, Jesus' consciousness of the *nearness* of the Kingdom is a feature that cannot be disposed of. Protestant theology, however, generally regards its task to be that of framing a unified Christian view of the world and life, which is supposed to be authoritative both for the individual and for all people for a long time to come. It would, therefore, at least have to mitigate the ardent eschatological tone of Jesus' proclamation. Thus it is explained first, that although the Kingdom of God has secondary significance for us as the "heavenly Kingdom of Completion," we should think of it primarily as the invisible community of men who venture to honor God as their King and Father and seek to obtain the effectiveness and extension of his rule among themselves and others by fulfillment of his will.

A new point of view concerning both the ideas of Jesus and dogmatics has recently been attempted: specifically by J. Kaftan, who in his volume on *Das Wesen der christlichen Religion*[96] represents the Kingdom of God even in Jesus' preaching less as a "community of men" than as the highest "religious good." Kaftan stresses,[97] quite correctly, against Reischle among others, that the dominant idea in Jesus' proclamation is "not that of a Kingdom of ethical righteousness in the world, but that of a superworldly, transcendent Kingdom of Blessedness." With this Kaftan contrasts the Kingdom of God as "supreme ethical ideal"; as such it is "inner worldly and its actualization a matter involving human initiative [*Selbstthätigkeit*]." After all that we have previously said, we can recognize that this conception is incorrect. The actualization of the Kingdom of God is *not* a matter for human initiative, but entirely a matter of God's initiative. The only thing man can do about it is to perform the conditions required by God. The Kingdom of God, in Jesus' view, is never an ethical ideal, but is *nothing other than the highest religious Good,* a Good which God grants on certain conditions. This does not imply a pharisaic conception of reward, but naturally only a person who is entirely detached from αἰὼν οὗτος can really possess and enjoy this Good in the Kingdom of God. Otherwise he lacks completely the proper spiritual disposition; hence, participa-

96. 2nd ed., [Basel: C. Detloff's Buchhandlung, 1888], pp. 236 ff.
97. [Kaftan, *Das Wesen,* p. 239. The reference is to Max Reischle, *Ein Wort zur Controverse über die Mystik in der Theologie* (Freiburg im Breisgau: Mohr [Siebeck], 1886), pp. 40–43.]

tion in this Kingdom corresponds only to that which is spiritually possible. This interpretation of the Kingdom of God as an innerworldly ethical ideal is a vestige of the Kantian idea and does not hold up before a more precise historical examination.

But modern notions easily creep in, even with the formula "the Kingdom of God is 'highest Good.' " On this point even Baldensperger[98] showed his bondage to the older dogmatic-exegetical method. He says,

> . . . the term Kingdom of God also designated that which Jesus, for his part, possessed already, what he felt in his own soul. His God-consciousness was so vivid that it awakened and confirmed his conviction that he lived in this Kingdom, or bore it in himself.

The linguistic form of this thesis alone (what does it mean: "to bear a Kingdom in oneself"?) can teach us that an undissolved dogmatic residue, something surprising in the case of Baldensperger, is present here. He obviously means the principal blessings which will be imparted to men in the messianic Kingdom—God's nearness and being completely a child of God—which Jesus already fully possessed. But this highest Good is certainly never connected with the expression "Kingdom of God." The Kingdom of God as Jesus thought of it is never something subjective, inward, or spiritual, but is always the objective messianic Kingdom, which usually is pictured as a territory into which one enters, or as a land in which one has a share, or as a treasure which comes down from heaven.[99]

98. Baldensperger, *Das Selbstbewusstsein Jesu*, pp. 132 ff.
99. According to Baldensperger, what is basically new in the preaching of Jesus is the shift from the category of *place* to that of *quality*. But this distinction is inadequate, because both are always present, side by side, in the idea of the Kingdom of God: the picture of a place and the Good, which includes many goods of a religious kind. The parables of the treasure and the pearl are as opposed to the meaning of a *present*

One must say, therefore, that the idea of the highest Good, which Kaftan has described with such eloquent words as the basic idea of Christianity, may not, strictly speaking, be tied to Jesus' idea of the Kingdom of God, for the latter signifies a still future and objective Good. Moreover, Jesus does not use the term "Kingdom of God" to refer to the "supreme ethical ideal," for the "righteousness" which he demanded is nothing but the condition for the future enjoyment of that objective Good.

For Jesus, the highest, present, personal Good is, instead, the consciousness of the love and care of the heavenly Father, *of being a child of God* [*die Gotteskindschaft*]. He himself lived in the enjoyment of this love, with a certainty and freshness which we cannot imitate, and also invited and instructed his disciples to lay hold of this highest Good in thankfulness and joy. The supreme ethical ideal is to serve God the Father with surrender of the whole heart, and to become free from the world. The highest proofs of this *freedom from the world* are *the love of one's enemy,* and *the sacrifice of one's life* for the sake of God. It is now possible indeed to embrace both of these sides of the Christian life under the inclusive category "Kingdom of God." This, then, would signify the invisible community established by Jesus and comprised of men who call upon God as Father and honor him as King. But then one will have to say more exactly, that *in the Kingdom of God* we have the highest Good, that of being children of God, and we earnestly endeavor to obtain the highest ethical ideal, that of perfectly fulfilling God's will. If one would like a *shorter* formulation, one might say (corresponding to the meaning of the word βασιλεία): the *Rule* of God is the highest religious Good and the supreme ethical ideal.

spiritual Good as they could be, for they teach that one must make sacrifice in order to reach *a still distant* Good.

But this conception of ours of the βασιλεία τοῦ θεοῦ parts company with Jesus' at the most decisive point. *We* do not mean the religious side of this concept antithetically, as the counterpart to αἰὼν οὗτος, but merely thetically: it expresses our belief that God the Creator maintains his control *over this world,* and governs it for the spiritual benefit of his children. Its ethical side is thoroughly unbiblical and un-Jewish, inasmuch as the notion of an "actualization of the Rule of God" by human ethical activity is completely contrary to the transcendentalism of Jesus' idea. Under these circumstances, one will perhaps judge the connection of the modern dogmatic idea with the words of Jesus to be a purely external one. This is, in fact, the case. That which is universally valid in Jesus' preaching, which should form the kernel of our systematic theology is not his idea of the Kingdom of God, but that of the religious and ethical fellowship of the children of God. This is not to say that one ought no longer to use the concept "Kingdom of God" in the current manner. On the contrary, it seems to me, as a matter of fact, that it should be the proper watchword of modern theology. Only the admission must be demanded that we use it in a different sense from Jesus'.

The real difference between our modern Protestant world-view and that of primitive Christianity is, therefore, that we do not share the eschatological attitude, namely, that τὸ σχῆμα τοῦ κόσμου τούτου παράγει. We no longer pray, "May grace come and the world pass away," but we pass our lives in the joyful confidence that *this* world will evermore become the showplace of the people of God. But another attitude has silently come among us in place of the strictly eschatological one—and where it is not present, preaching and instruction should do all they can to awaken it. The world will further endure, but we, as individuals, will soon leave it. Thereby, we will at least approximate

Jesus' attitude in a different sense, if we make the basis of our life the precept spoken by a wise man of our day: "Live as if you were dying." We do not await a Kingdom of God which is to come down from heaven to earth and abolish this world, but we do hope to be gathered with the church of Jesus Christ into the heavenly βασιλεία. In this sense we, too, can feel and say, as did the Christians of old: "Thy Kingdom come!"[100]

100. We would call attention here once more (see above, p. 97) to the fact that this transformation of the idea of the Kingdom of God is perhaps already very ancient. As early as in the Jewish-Christian source of Luke, which contains the parable of poor Lazarus, the episode of the thief on the cross and perhaps also the saying in Acts 14:22, the idea seems to be present that when the faithful and righteous die, they are directly transported into the messianic Kingdom, which is in Paradise or Heaven. To be sure, the idea of the return of the Son of man was also retained along with this.

[In *Predigt²*, Weiss attributes the sayings in Luke about the immediate fate of Lazarus and the thief (16:22 f.; 23:43) to Jesus himself. He explains the former as follows: "Jesus' thought, like popular thought about such matters was unsystematic" (p. 113). Jesus had in mind the Isaianic prophecies, e.g., Is. 65:13–25 and 35:10 (pp. 117 f.). The thief, he considers, was a special case. Jesus will take him directly to the place where the righteous and elect are to have their ultimate dwelling (*Enoch* 39:6, 7), not to any intermediate place (cf. John 14:2 f.), (pp. 113 f.). Weiss makes no reference to "Luke's Ebionite source" in his discussion of these verses in the second edition. Cf. above, p. 99, n. 65. He observes that Paul also expected that some, including himself, might go directly from life on earth to life with the Lord: cf. 2 Cor. 5.4–10; Phil. 1:23; 1 Thess. 4:16 f. He proposes that the two views may be unified through the perspective expressed in *Enoch* 38:1 ff., in which the assembly of the righteous in heaven (cf. Heb. 12:23) will appear together with the Messiah at the time when those righteous and elect who are still on earth are judged and separated from the sinners (pp. 114 f.).]

BIBLIOGRAPHY
AND
INDEXES

BIBLIOGRAPHY OF THE
MAJOR WRITINGS OF
JOHANNES WEISS

1888

Der Barnabasbrief kritisch untersucht mit besonderer Berücksichtigung seiner Beurteiling des Alten Testaments und seines Verhältnisses zu den neutestamentlichen Schriften. Göttingen: Neu-Ruppin (Inaugural Dissertation).

1890

"Die Verteidigung Jesu gegen den Vorwurf des Bündnisses mit Beelzebul." *TSK* 63, pp. 555–69.

"Nothwendige Reformen in der evangelischen Kirche." *Deutsche Wochenbericht* 3, pp. 334 f.; 345–47; 360–62.

1891

"Die Parabelrede bei Marcus." *Studien und Kritiken*, pp. 289–321.

1892

Die Evangelien des Markus und Lukas, with B. Weiss (Meyers Kommentar). Göttingen: Vandenhoeck & Ruprecht.

Frauenberuf. Ein Beitrag zur Frauenfrage. (Evangelisch-soziale Zeitfragen, 2. Reihe, Heft 7), Leipzig: Grunow.

"Die Komposition der synoptischen Wiederkunftsrede." *Studien und Kritiken,* pp. 246–270.

Die Predigt Jesu vom Reiche Gottes. Göttingen: Vandenhoeck & Ruprecht. Second revised edition: 1900. Third edition.

edited and with an introduction by Ferdinand Hahn, with an accompanying note by Rudolf Bultmann: 1964.

1893

"Das Judenchristentum in der Apostelgeschichte." *TSK* 66, pp. 480–540.

1895

Die Nachfolge Christi und die Predigt der Gegenwart. Göttingen: Vandenhoeck & Ruprecht.

"Paulinische Probleme. Die Chronologie der Paulinischen Briefe." *TSK* 68, pp. 252–96.

"Paulinische Probleme II. Die Formel ἐν Χριστῷ Ἰησοῦ." *TSK* 69, pp. 7–33.

"Apostelgeschichte und apostolisches Zeitalter." *Theologische Rundschau* 1 (1897-98), pp. 371–77.

1897

Beiträge zur paulinischen Rhetorik. Göttingen: Vandenhoeck & Ruprecht. (This short work also appeared in *Theologische Studien: Herrn Wirkl. Oberkonsistorialrath Prof. Dr. Bernhard Weiss zu seinem 70. Geburtstage dargebracht.* Göttingen: Vandenhoeck & Ruprecht, 1897, pp. 165–247.)

"Neue Logia." *Theologische Rundschau* 1 (1897-98), pp. 227–36.

Ueber die Absicht und den literarischen Charakter der Apostelgeschichte. Göttingen: Vandenhoeck & Ruprecht.

1898

"Dämonen" and "Dämonische" in Hauck's *Realencyklopädie für protestantische Theologie und Kirche,* third edition, Leipzig: Hinrichs, Bd. 4, pp. 408–19.

1900

"Der Eingang des ersten Korintherbriefes." *TSK* 13, pp. 357–62.

Die Predigt Jesu vom Reiche Gottes. Göttingen: Vandenhoeck & Ruprecht. Second revised edition.

1901

Die Idee des Reiches Gottes in der Theologie. Giessen: J. Ricker.

1902

Die christliche Freiheit nach der Verkündigung des Apostels Paulus. Göttingen: Vandenhoeck & Ruprecht.

1903

Das älteste Evangelium. Ein Beitrag zum Verständnis des Markusevangeliums und der ältesten evangelischen Ueberlieferung. Göttingen: Vandenhoeck & Ruprecht.

1904

Die Offenbarung des Johannes. Ein Beitrag zur literatur- und Religionsgeschichte. Göttingen: Vandenhoeck & Ruprecht.

1905

"Wellhausens Evangelienkommentar." *Theologische Rundschau* 8, pp. 1–9.

1906

Articles in James Hastings, *A Dictionary of Christ and the Gospels.* New York: Scribner's:

"Acts of the Apostles" vol. 1, pp. 25–28

"Ethics" vol. 1, pp. 543–47

"King" vol. 1, pp. 931 f.

"Passion Week" vol. 2, pp. 323 ff.

Die Schriften des Neuen Testaments, neu übersetzt und erklärt (in collaboration with Hermann Gunkel, Wilhelm Bousset, Wilhelm Heitmüller, and others; Weiss was general editor and was responsible for the Synoptics and Revelation in particular), 2d edition, 1913.

1908

Die Aufgaben der neutestamentlichen Wissenschaft in der Gegenwart. Göttingen: Vandenhoeck & Ruprecht.

1909

Christus. Die Anfänge des Dogmas. Tübingen: J.C.B. Mohr (Paul Siebeck). Trans. V. D. David, *Christ: the Beginnings of Dogma.* Boston: American Unitarian Association, 1911.

Paulus und Jesus. Berlin: Reuther & Reichard. Trans. H. J. Chaynor, *Paul and Jesus.* London and New York: Harper.

1910

Der erste Korintherbrief (Meyer Kommentar, 9. Auflage). Göttingen: Vandenhoeck & Ruprecht.

"ΕΥΘΥΣ bei Markus." *ZNW* 11, pp. 124–33.

Die Geschichtlichkeit Jesu (with Georg Grützmacher). Tübingen: J.C.B. Mohr (Paul Siebeck).

Jesus im Glauben des Urchristentums. Tübingen: J.C.B. Mohr (Paul Siebeck).

Jesus von Nazareth: Mythus oder Geschichte? Eine Auseinandersetzung mit Kalthoff, Drews, Jenson. Tübingen: J.C.B. Mohr (Paul Siebeck).

"Zum Märtyrertod der Zebedäiden." *ZNW* 11, p. 167.

"Zum reichen Jüngling, (Mark 10:13–17)." *ZNW* 11, pp. 79–83.

1912

Ueber die Kraft. Björnsons Drama und das religiöse Problem. Tübingen: J.C.B. Mohr (Paul Siebeck).

"Das Herrenmahl der Urgemeinde." *Protestantische Monatshefte* 16, pp. 53–60.

1913

"Das Problem der Entstehung des Christentums." *Archiv für Religionswissenschaft* 16, pp. 423–515.

"The Significance of Paul for Modern Christians." *American Journal of Theology* 17, pp. 352–67. (Published posthumously in *ZNW* 19 [1919–20], pp. 127–42).

Synoptische Tafeln zu den drei älteren Evangelien mit Unterscheidung der Quellen in vierfachem Farbendruck. Göttingen: Vandenhoeck & Ruprecht. 2d edition, 1920.

1914

Das Urchristentum. Göttingen: Vandenhoeck & Ruprecht. Trans. four friends, ed. F. C. Grant, *The History of Primitive Christianity.* New York: Erickson, 1937. Reprinted: New York: Harper, 1959 (2 vol. Paperback).

Weiss's conversations with other scholars working on the Synoptics can be traced in *Theologische Rundschau:*

vol.	1 (1897–98)	pp. 288–97
	2 (1899)	pp. 140–52
	4 (1901)	pp. 148–61
	6 (1903)	pp. 199–211
	11 (1908)	pp. 92–105, 122–33
	16 (1913)	pp. 183–96, 219–25

Weiss also wrote on a wide range of popular topics; see, e.g., *Christ und Welt* 8 (1894), 11 (1897), 12 (1898).

INDEX OF SCRIPTURE REFERENCES

144

INDEX OF NAMES

Type, 11 on 12 and 10 on 11 Garamond
Display, Garamond